# Singapore
## towards the year 2000

6/108)
A + R
X - 41

# *Singapore*
## *towards the Year 2000*

Edited by
Saw Swee-Hock
and R.S. Bhathal

Published by Singapore University Press
for the Singapore Association for the
Advancement of Science

Printed by Welco Printers Pte. Ltd., Singapore.

# Contents

Preface       vii

1. Political Developments towards the Year 2000       1
   *S. Rajaratnam*

2. The Emerging Administrative State       10
   *Chan Heng Chee*

3. Too Little Land, Too Many People       15
   *Saw Swee-Hock*

4. Planning the Economy for a Surprise-free Future       34
   *Pang Eng Fong*

5. The Relationship between Political Parties and Trade       44
   Unions in the Context of Economic Development
   *Lim Chee Onn*

6. Images of Man-made Environment       63
   *Liu Thai Ker*

7. Impact of Technological Changes and Developments       87
   *R. S. Bhathal*

8. Energy Options and Their Implications       94
   *Tay Sin-Yan*

9. Limits to Medicine       106
   *Wong Hock Boon*

10. Whither the Fine Arts?       131
    *Chia Wai Hon*

11. Cultural Change and Social Values       140
    *Ho Wing Meng*

12. Towards a Creative Society       156
    *William S. W. Lim*

Notes on Contributors       163

# Contents

Preface .......... vii

# Preface

*Singapore towards the Year 2000* comprises the revised versions of the papers presented at a seminar bearing the same title and organized by the Singapore Association for the Advancement of Science and the Singapore Science Centre in December 1979. The objectives of the seminar were (1) to assess the present policies, their potential changes and implications in the fields of politics, economics, sociology, and technology as Singapore moves forward in the next two decades; (2) to create an awareness among our people about the options open to us and the likely changes and their consequences that may occur in the future; (3) to seek and formulate some guidelines for our progress towards the year 2000. The contributors to this book were urged to take these objectives into consideration in preparing their original papers for presentation at the seminar and in revising them for publication.

On behalf of the Association we would like to thank the members of the Advisory Panel and the Organizing Committee of the seminar, the Shell Companies in Singapore for sponsoring the seminar, and the Minister for Foreign Affairs, Mr. S. Rajaratnam, for delivering the keynote address. We would also like to thank the Shell Companies of Singapore for providing a generous grant which has made the publication of this book possible.

December 1980                          Saw Swee-Hock and R. S. Bhathal

# 1

# Political Developments towards the Year 2000

## S. Rajaratnam

I think I should begin by declaring what vested interest, if any, I have in the Singapore of the year 2000. Regrettably I have none. I may not be around to ring in the new century, but if through a genetic windfall I should be given a reprieve, you may be sure that even then for all practical purposes I will be nearer eternity than the year 2000.

I mention this somewhat bleak prospect not because it would have any great consequence for twenty-first century history but merely to impress on you the unquestioned objectivity with which I shall approach the subject you have set out for me — political developments towards the year 2000.

Let me at the outset clarify my views on speculations about the future. There are practical men who maintain that such speculations are a waste of time and they have no bearing at all on solutions to immediate day-to-day problems. This may have been so in earlier periods of history when changes were few and minute and were spread over decades and centuries. The day-to-day problems that the son had to tackle were not basically different from those that his father or even his grandfather had to cope with.

Therefore, in earlier societies the passing of time was experienced in a two-dimensional way — the past and the present. This was an advance on a still earlier period, as in primitive societies today, when men lived in a timeless world. People lived only for the moment. They had no sense of the past unless it was a legendary past of mythical heroes and improbable gods.

That is why mankind has been able to get along for centuries without clocks and time-pieces. A consciousness of history, in the sense we understand it today, is a new experience for mankind — perhaps not more than two or three thousand years old. Even then in this two-dimensional view of history, the past took priority over the present. You turned to the past for precedents and inspiration to help resolve the problems of the present. Most societies were tradition bound. Any departure from the old way of doing things was viewed with abhorrence and apprehension. And in times of troubles and uncertainty the prescription offered was a return to a Golden Age which lay in the past and from which men had strayed. This view of history is essentially pessimistic because it forecloses the possibility of a new Golden Age in the future. A step forward into the future is one more towards damnation. Only by returning to the past can one find assurance and safety.

This two-dimensional experience of time, whatever validity it may have had in the past, cannot help us with the problems of the coming centuries. Mankind has entered a phase of history radically different in all its essentials from preceding periods of history. One of the distinctive facts about contemporary history is that it is world history, and that the forces shaping it cannot be understood unless we are prepared to adopt worldwide perspectives. Not only should contemporary history be considered a distinct period of time with characteristics unlike any we have known before but we must also add a new dimension to the concept of time if we are to deal effectively with day-to-day problems. This three-dimensional awareness of time is necessary and vital because we are living in a world of accelerating change, of changes which are global in scope and which permeate almost all aspects of human activity. The consequences of change can flow only in one direction — towards the future. It cannot affect the past because the past is beyond change. We may turn to it to guide future actions, and this we must do because it can offer us many valuable lessons — what errors men of earlier times made, why at times they created civilizations that still overawe us, and why succeeding generations were reduced to scrambling about their ruins unable even to tell us what the ancestral civilizations were all about.

Since change is about the future, then only a future-oriented society can cope with the problems of the twenty-first century. You must learn to cope with day-to-day problems, not in terms of the present or the past but of the future. The present too, like the past, is unchangeable. What has happened has happened and there is nothing you can do about it. What is more important is what you are going to do about the consequences of what has already happened.

The practical man would say, "Let us think about the immediate conseqences and let tomorrow take care of itself." This, in my view, is not a practical approach because in the kind of world we live in, the consequences are of infinite duration and *ad hoc* solutions without long-range calculations are a gambler's approach to human problems.

In thinking about the future we should approach it like a chess player rather than a gambler. The chess player plans his every move by thinking many steps ahead. A one-move chess player is out by the time he makes his second move.

i admit that the game of life is far more complicated than a chess game. In the game of life the chess pieces run into billions and unlike chess-men the pieces that make up the life game have unpredictable wills of their own. Therefore, in the real world, thinking many steps ahead cannot be precise as in chess. This comes very close to fortune telling and prediction and no genius, not even a super-computer, can predict what the consequences of an action or an event would be five, ten, or twenty years from now.

On the other hand, I do not subscribe to the view that the consequences are totally capricious and that we cannot make informed guesses about their general drift. We do it most of the time, for if there were not some measure of predictability about what human beings would do tomorrow or even the next year all societies would be in a state of total anarchy.

So while thinking many steps ahead may not always ensure success, it is nevertheless true that those societies which think many steps ahead are more likely to do better in the uncertain decades ahead than others which only think one step at a time or which, frightened by the future, take one step back towards the lost and irrecoverable Golden Age. In a small and modest way, Singapore has demonstrated the efficacy of thinking many steps ahead, of thinking in terms of the future than of the past. Of course we are fortunate in that Singapore has no Golden Age to lure it away from the future. If there were such Golden Ages then we must inevitably trace them back to India or China or Indonesia, and since we have decided to be Singaporeans we can do this only surreptitiously and without great feeling behind it.

So we are stuck only with a future and a conscious past starting from 1819. And as a nation we are only fourteen years old. The absence of a Golden Age has, of course, its drawbacks when we confront others with a lineage which can be reckoned in centuries. That is why when a curious visitor asks Singaporeans for a brief summary of their national history, the visitor may be surprised to find the summary briefer than he expected.

The only consolation I can offer is that the Singaporean of the year 2000 can be a little more long-winded about Singapore's past. If all goes well he would be talking not about a dead society but of a living, dynamic, and thriving community of peoples who have successfully coped with the challenges of the twenty-first century and who are still future oriented.

So this brings me to the next and most crucial question implicit in the topic you have set out for me: Granted that Singapore is future-oriented, is that enough to see it through into the twenty-first century?

My answer is: No, it is not enough. Something far more important than being able to make informed guesses about the future is necessary to see Singapore safely through the turbulent and dangerous decades ahead. Even if you can make correct guesses about future trends and developments, and even if you stumble on the correct solutions, the decisive factor is not knowledge but the determination and courage to act upon them. Without this will to action, knowledge and perception about the future are useless. There are nations which have perished because they did not know how to save themselves. It is a tragedy when a nation perishes not out of ignorance but because they lacked the will to respond to the dictates of their wisdom.

The rise and fall of great civilizations can eventually be traced not to irresistible, impersonal forces of history but to a single human factor — failure of nerve.

Here I must turn to the past for guidance on this matter, to those great thinkers who had watched with dismay, sorrow, or anger the un- necessary disintegration of their civilizations — Plato, Confucius, Thucydides, the Jewish Prophets, and Machiavelli, to name a few. All of them tried desperately to educate their rulers on how to cope with the problem of change, the crises of their times. Their rulers proved, alas, to be incorrigible students.

Machiavelli, in the sixteenth century, deeply concerned by the strife and turbulence of petty tyrants who were undermining the greatness of Florence, offered the following advice to a Saviour Prince. He said all societies were moved by two forces. He distinguished between what he called *fortuna* — the capriciousness of history — and *virtu* — the ability of a ruler to show mastery amidst the flux of things. *Fortuna* comprises the objective forces of history stemming from economic, social, cultural, political, and technological changes. These are like winds. They are un- predictable; they are impersonal; and they can be destructive.

But rulers who have *virtu* can harness and tame these winds to serve men's needs, to build greater civilizations. The presence or loss of *virtu* in rulers and people decides the fate of societies and civilizations.

So the question arises: "How is *virtu* acquired and lost?" This fun- damental question has fascinated thinkers since time immemorial. Un- able to resolve this question, they invariably pinned responsibility on the Creator. It was punishment for men's wickedness — and this view has wide appeal even today in the face of a contemporary world seem- ingly near collapse.

I too have been thinking about this problem since receiving your invitation to address this seminar. I happened at the same time to be also thinking about Ayatollah Khomeiny. Since the Ayatollah claims to be spearheading an Islamic Revolution I decided to supplement my meagre knowledge of Islamic civilization by studying its rise and fall a little more closely. I therefore sought the advice of Professor Hussein Alatas who promptly lent me a massive three-volume work entitled *Muquaddimah: An Introduction to History.*

I was doubtful whether it would be worth ploughing through these massive tomes. For one thing it was written by a man called Ibn Khaldoun whom I had never heard of and who is rarely mentioned by modern historians. Moreover the work was completed in 1377. Of what relevance, I asked myself, could the outpourings of a man from over six centuries ago be to our times, let alone the year 2000.

I was never more wrong in my life. This fourteenth-century Berber, a descendant of one of the Prophet's supporters, is so contemporary that many modern historians in comparison appear traditional. The Ayatollah is certainly less of an enigma to me now than before I read Ibn Khaldoun, though I doubt whether the Ayatollah will be as relevant as Khaldoun in the year 2000. It is incredible that this fourteenth-century man should have anticipated ideas about man and society, about jurisprudence, geopolitics, power, religion, war and peace, and many of the great themes about the rise and fall of civilizations centuries before thinkers like Vico, Marx, Spengler, and Toynbee elaborated them with greater wealth of detail.

The wrappings which conceal his basic ideas are admittedly medieval and unacceptable to modern minds. He accepts the conventional wisdoms of his time. We must remember too that in his time Islamic civilization was dominant in Europe and Africa. The Muslim faith, philosophy, and law made up the tower from which he points out to his contemporaries and to us new and wider horizons which no man before or even after him had discovered until very recently. He nevertheless looks on his environment with a detachment and objectivity that was not to be surpassed until centuries later by Western man. He states facts. He observes. He knows the glorious past of his own civilization. He knows the Caliphate represented the best, the ideal state. But he is aware too that it is gone and he does not want to restore it. He concedes that government based on revealed law is superior to that based on human law. This may be obvious, he says, but it is irrelevant for history moves according to the ways of men and not of god.

What then has Ibn Khaldoun to say about the rise and fall of civilizations that is relevant to us. It is difficult to summarize his thoughts on this without making them sound banal. It is like trying to whistle a symphony. His volumes are as rich and various, as subtle, deep, and formless as the ocean from which one fishes ideas sometimes too quaint for our tastes and often startlingly modern.

He allots to all civilizations a finite life-span of about 120 years spread over three generations of forty years each. In the fourth generation the end is reached. And by the fifth the final death spasms.

He says that this is the invariable and predictable course of history, though sometimes he seems to offer an escape. For why, he asks, has civilization proved to be so much stronger in the East than in the West, in Persia and Iraq, Syria and Egypt, than in the Maghreb which was the focus for his great work. He had also seen the merchants of Europe who came to the Barbary ports and had marvelled at their wealth and splendid way of life. He did not pursue this fertile path, for had he done so he might have guessed that Western Europe would soon light its torch of civilization from the glowing embers of Islamic culture.

What sparks off a civilization in the first place? He attributes it to a special human quality which he calls *"asabiyya"*. It means group solidarity, but it takes different forms and meanings at different stages of civilization. It is initially generated only in the desert. In the Arab context it had to be the desert since at the time of Ibn Khaldoun, Damascus had already fallen to the Mongol conqueror, Tamarlane — also a man of the desert. But in Europe the barbarians poured out from its forests and icy wastes.

What Khaldoun means is that *asabiyya* has to be built up through hardship and great austerity. That is why, says Khaldoun, the Prophet Moses deliberately kept the Israelites whom he had led out of Egypt for forty years in the desert. As slaves in Egypt the Israelites had become subservient and fatalistic. They had been drained of *asabiyya*. It took a generation of exposure to the hardships of the desert to renew their *asabiyya*. In more modern times, it was in Hitler's ghettos that the Israelites of today built up *asabiyya*. It was in the desert too that the Prophet Mohammed conjured up the *asabiyya* which inspired the great Islamic conquests. Though Ibn Khaldoun wrote of the nomads with detestation as destroyers of culture and not its creators he admired their *asabiyya* — their courage, toughness, their self-reliance, and above all their solidarity and fellowship.

The men with *asabiyya,* headed by a great leader or prophet, then take over a dying civilization and thus begins a sedentary culture — a city culture. Khaldoun makes clear that while the desert generates *asabiyya* only the city can create civilization. As long as the spirit of *asabiyya* prevails, the first-generation ruler exercises power justly and wisely. The law is fairly applied. Taxation policies are designed to stimulate prosperity and personal initiative. The ruler, says Khaldoun, does not claim anything exclusively for himself because such an attitude is what is required by group solidarity. With this kind of ruler, order prevails and art and learning flourish. Out of the ashes of the old civilization a greater and more vibrant culture emerges.

The next four stages are stages of progressive decline. The easy democracy of the first stage vanishes as the new ruler claims total authority over his people. Authority is no longer shared. He becomes a tyrant demanding subjects who must manifest servility and unquestioned obedience. The *asabiyya* is being drained out of them. Discontent and resentment dissolve group solidarity. The tyrant is succeeded by vainglorious rulers also lacking in *asabiyya*. They build monuments and palaces to testify to nothing. They hire mercenaries to protect themselves from a people they now fear and no longer trust. Nepotism and corruption become the rule of law. The burden of taxation grows and incentive for creation of wealth consequently dies. Then comes the ruler "who is content with what his predecessors have built". Since his civilization has lost its capacity for growth, the ruler tries to arrest its decline by reviving and adhering strictly to old rituals and meaningless traditions.

And finally the death pangs of a great civilization. Here I can do no better than quote Khaldoun himself:

> The fifth stage is one of waste and squandering. In this stage the ruler wastes on pleasures and amusements (the treasures) accumulated by his ancestors through (excessive) generosity to his inner circle at their parties. Also he acquires bad, low class followers to whom he entrusts the most important matters (of state) which they are not qualified to handle by themselves.... (In addition) the ruler seeks to destroy the great clients of his people and followers of his predecessors. Thus they come to hate him and to conspire to refuse support to him. (Furthermore) he loses a number of soldiers by spending their allowances on his pleasures and by refusing them access to his person and not supervising them properly.... Thus he ruins the foundations his ancestors had laid and tears down what they had built up. In this stage the dynasty is seized by senility and the chronic disease from which it can hardly ever rid itself, for which it can find no cure, and, eventually, it is destroyed.

He might well be describing with deadly accuracy the state of many nations in 1979.

He goes on to add that the end of the dynasty is clearly in sight when the hard-up ruler, unable to squeeze his subjects any further, takes part in trade and commerce and tries to monopolize it to the detriment of his trading subjects.

By then the *asabiyya,* bred in the desert, has been drained of its last drop. The city, the soil of true civilization, has become a wasteland.

What happens then? A new lot of desert nomads bursting with *asabiyya* take over the dying city to once again restore vigour and once again to suffer the same fate.

In a way Singapore was built by nomads, though none of us came from the desert. Our forefathers had *asabiyya* and this has seen us through for a little over the 120 years that Khaldoun allotted a dynasty. On second thought he was not all that wrong because it took that many years for the British dynasty to retreat from Singapore.

So in a manner of speaking, Singapore's destiny is in the hands of only the first generation of rulers. It is today prosperous and dynamic. But as Khaldoun warns, the comforts, distractions, and ease that a prosperous city offers its peoples and rulers can exhaust the *asabiyya* so necessary to nourish it.

Khaldoun says that there is no way of bringing about a fruitful coexistence between a city civilization and *asabiyya* — civic solidarity. *Asabiyya* is also Machiavelli's *virtu.* At the heart of both lies the question of human will. Despite Khaldoun's assertion to the contrary it can be bred, I think, in cities as well as in the desert. Khaldoun's dismal cycle can be broken if the people so will it.

In any case, we are not today dealing as Khaldoun had to with an isolated regional civilization but with a world civilization. World civilization is too pervasive for it to collapse and vanish totally. In the twenty-first century, there may be collapse of individual states which have not woken up to the facts of life about the twenty-first century. But those who are awake to it and do not squander their *asabiyya* or *virtu* in the pursuit of wealth and progress can break the circle that Khaldoun said could not be broken but had at times wished that it would be.

By telling us in his enthralling introduction to history how and why civilization suffers mortality he has also offered a prescription for its immortality. If you know why you went wrong you come closer to doing things right.

The next two decades are going to be for Singapore, as for the rest of the world, years of uncertainty and turmoil. So it was for Ibn Khaldoun and for humanity ever since it went in for civilization building. As far as I can see: civilization building has really never stopped. Only its builders and architects have changed from time to time.

For Singapore the next two decades will be a matter of learning to steer safely through *fortuna* — the capricious play of world forces. To steer successfully we need what Machiavelli called *virtu,* what Khaidoun called *asabiyya* and, if I may add my widow's mite, a future-oriented outlook.

Given the qualities I see no reason why Singapore should not find its way successfully into the twenty-first century. And if some time during that century I should happen to run across Ibn Khaldoun in that time-less region, I think he would be delighted to hear from me that his vicious circle had at last been broken.

If not I shall most certainly avoid him.

# 2

# The Emerging Administrative State

## Chan Heng Chee

In the year 2000, Mr. Lee Kuan Yew will be 76, Dr. Goh Keng Swee will be 82, Mr. Rajaratnam will be 85, and Mr. Goh Chok Tong will be 3 years older than what the Prime Minister is today. Singapore may be governed by a gerontocracy, or we may be run by a team of very young systems engineers.

I must make it clear that I speak with no special background in futurology and I am much more confident when generalizing in retrospect than in prospect.

*Retrospect and Prospect*

In retrospect, we shall have to recognize that the most important political development in Singapore since its independence has been the emergence of an administrative state. I first conceptualized the politics of Singapore as an administrative state in 1975. Since then, the internal political developments have convinced me that I am along the right track and have provided me with further data to refine and understand this model of a political system.

Let me briefly recapitulate the ideological bases and features of the administrative state as I argued the theory in 1975. Political leaders who favour the establishment of an administrative state look upon government and politics as an exercise of state management, and firmly believe that society is better off if its problems are resolved through a rational application of scientific techniques to the sources of the problems, and if resources can be allocated according to a centralized coordinated programme rather than through autonomous political bargaining. In Singapore we have seen these ideological assumptions expressed in the style of governance and the concomitant depoliticization in the political arena. Confrontational politics and the politics of competitive mobilization and bargain are discouraged and viewed as destabilizing. The distinctive features of such a state would be:

1. The power of the bureaucratic sector would be increased because of the rise of complex organizations and the proliferation of develop-

mental activities in the society, particularly those undertaken by governmental enterprises.

2. The importance of the elected politician's role *vis-a-vis* the bureaucrat would be reduced because in a non-competitive political arena, his contribution to the party's survival strength is not crucial. The mobilizer is not as esteemed as the technocrat in an administrative state. MPs are however important as transmitters of grassroots thinking.

3. The style of government looks for the elimination of politics and places trust on experts and expertise in planning and implementation.

Today I would make one modification to this thesis and elaborate further on the workings of this model. My statement about the importance of the bureaucrat's position *vis-a-vis* that of the Members of Parliament needs refinement. I am not arguing that bureaucrats have usurped power from the politicians. Parliament in Singapore is supreme and the cabinet leadership is very much supreme, but below the level of cabinet ministers and deputy ministers, the weight and scope of power of the MPs are far less than those of the top civil servants who are entrusted with wide powers by the elected government.

It is also a corollary development of the administrative state that the civil service is seen to be the recruiting ground for political leadership and civil servants are moved with ease by the ruling party into the political arena. The senior bureaucrats have attained such prominence and share in the responsibility and exercise of power so widely that they are regarded as the natural allies and successors to political leadership. The transfer of the bureaucrat to the political arena should cause no disruption and indeed is seen as a logical process. The only adjustment that must be made is the development of grassroots links of the bureaucrat-turned-politician, and in a highly organized and structured political system such as ours, this may not be particularly difficult to effect. In 1975, when I spoke of the administrative state, this transfer was not yet apparent. The major influx of bureaucrats into politics came in the 1976 General Elections, the 1977 bye-elections, and the 1979 bye-elections; in future we shall see more civil servants in political positions.

It should also come as no surprise to us that the stress on the public sector has been so explicit in recent times as the administrative state takes root. The Government is committed to building a premier corps of administrators by attracting the best brains to the state bureaucracy with the right pay and quick promotion, although it does not set out to hog all the talent — it is prepared to allow two-thirds of the top talent to spearhead the private sector (see Mr. Goh Chok Tong's announcements, 15 March 1979).

Some concern has been expressed over this trend of putting so many bureaucrats into politics. Firstly, it is feared that we may be losing too many first-rate, experienced administrators (furthermore, they may turn out to be second-rate politicians and that would represent a loss indeed). Secondly, there is some doubt that appointed leaders are as effective in times of crises as leaders who are thrown from the ranks. Can they galvanize and mobilize the people? For then it will be important to mobilize. Let us hope so. The more I think on this matter the more I am convinced that this doubt can never be clarified. In a sense it is a useless question to ask if the successor bureaucratic leadership will be as successful as the present leadership. The answer is, we cannot really tell. If Mr. X who succeeds Mr. Lee Kuan Yew decides to adopt policy B instead of policy A, we cannot tell if this is worse or better than what Mr. Lee would have chosen, because we would not know what Mr. Lee would have chosen. We have no means of comparative evaluation. Besides, all leaders make mistakes in the course of their governance. The present leaders have admitted to some of their mistakes. The point is that if the political mistakes are small enough, you can criticize and amend the mistakes and that is normal in the course of running a country. If the political mistake is really monumental, it then becomes history, and I think the reason why history takes certain courses depends on many variables, sometimes not totally the result of actions taken by one or two decision-makers. For Singapore the external environment yields too many uncontrolled variables.

*Prospect*

As Singapore moves towards the year 2000, one internal political issue that will arise and affect other issues is how we resolve the contradiction between the need for greater control and the need for greater participation, in all spheres. It is clear that we are moving into an era that calls for greater control. Towards the year 2000, Singapore, an island of 616 square kilometres will be confronted with a tight population situation. The population projections have ranged from 2.7 million to 3 million (*Population and Trends*, Singapore: Ministry of Health, 1977) — nearly a million more — not to mention the one million or more tourists who will be sharing the services and infrastructure with the local population. As it stands, our population density is 3,929 per square kilometre, which is one of the highest in the world. The inescapable logic is that to co-exist more or less in an orderly civilized manner, greater planning, regulation, and control of activities and lifestyle will be necessary. In all likelihood, energy will certainly be dearer and scarcer unless a cheap alternative is tapped soon. Let's hope we will not have to put up with rationing queues and that the spread effect of dearer oil does not generate run-away inflation.

When the Prime Minister launched the courtesy campaign in June 1979, he was already anticipating this problem, and the slogan "courtesy to make life more pleasant" aims at more than a surface objective. His statement that "greater courtesy will help us to be psychologically better adjusted with less pent up frustration" reveals the more serious purpose of promoting courtesy, for if the citizenry can internalize ways and manners which can help us to co-exist pleasantly and harmoniously together in a crowded environment, we minimize the control that may otherwise be needed externally.

Apart from the internal physical factors which will affect us and which we can predict as a consequence of our demographic change, there will be the less predictable external factors which will affect domestic developments such as the regional political developments which will affect the investment climate if we are unfortunate enough not to have peace. The leaders will feel, more than ever before, that it may be necessary to implement unpopular policies. This prospect is already evident in the tone of the current speeches of the political leaders, and, given the projection of international and regional events, the ability of the next generation of leaders to analyse and define political situations and to communicate them to the people is all-important.

Yet there is also the other development — the emergence of a literate, basically English-educated population. The swing to English is a fact. In 1978 the Primary I enrolment showed that 88.6 per cent of the students were enrolled in the English stream and 11.15 per cent in the Chinese stream. This year, the figure for the Chinese stream is 9 per cent, according to Dr. Goh Keng Swee (Nanyang Convocation). Looking at our education statistics we will find that in the year 2000, of the age group 30 and below, at least 90 per cent will be English-educated. In the age group 30—40 years, roughly 71 per cent are English-educated. Furthermore, the policy in education is to avoid attrition and to improve the quality of education. If these trends are maintained, we can predict a growth of a literate and better-educated population tuned in to Western ideas and values and, if they are working men and women, to Western and Japanese models of management as well.

I believe, notwithstanding bilingualism and moral education, the sum exposure of the citizenry to Western films, television, and the cinema, Western books, Western journals, newspapers, pop songs, and the interaction with Western companies in trade and commerce, and travel will lead us to gravitate towards the West, and adopt Western values and attitudes (which are values identified with a modern, urban, and industrial environment). This will lead to a greater demand for participation. The political public, or that strata of intelligent, educated, and informed citizenry will be greater in the year 2000 than it is today, and they will want some form of participation in decisions that affect their lives. The pressure for participation will also come from Singaporeans in the year 2000, for most would have tasted material wealth. When material needs are satisfied people usually look for meaning in life. This meaning of course for some will be found in religion, but there will be those seeking participation. Notice, I have not jumped to the conclusion that there will be a greater demand for freedom, nor am I suggesting that the conditions would produce demands for a Western liberal democratic model.

The direction of development in Singapore will of necessity be different because of the historical experience and the socialization of Singaporeans into a political tradition nurtured under the administrative state. In Singapore there is a growing consensus that too much politics is destabilizing, and so long as the political leadership is doing reasonably well, it should be left to make the decisions. But, as I've said, there is also the other pull of education and exposure to Western values so that democracy is seen as something which is "a good" and which ought to be practised. The result is an ambiguity about democracy and what democratic politics entails. Eventually, this new demand for participation will be resolved in the search for new opportunities for people to be consulted and for them to express their views. It need not take the form of an outcry for opposition party politics. The need for expression is already evident in the letter columns of the English-language daily, the *Straits Times,* for recent letters reflect this new intelligent, critical mood. The letters no longer dwell on pipes, drains, and roads. Of course it may also be editorial policy which has made it possible to encourage more thoughtful issue-centred letters. Whatever it is, the letters reveal a sophistication and level of intelligent discussion that was not apparent a few years ago, for example, the letters on the "Speak Mandarin Campaign" and the firm but polite letters to ministers.

The mark of an educated person, and there will be more better educated persons in time to come, is his ability to focus his dissatisfaction and his aspirations and to translate them into words. This aspiration will not only be at the level of the middle class. The workers, who will also be better educated, will be an interesting category to watch. They will also demand participation and their right to express their opinions. The issue therefore is: how will the political leadership satisfy the need to participate, to create more channels for dialogue, and yet at the same time to meet the pressures for control and regulation?

# 3

## Too Little Land, Too Many People

**Saw Swee-Hock**

In this paper I shall present a brief review of the population control programme in Singapore, the impact of this programme on fertility levels and hence population growth, and the likely population trends in the future as Singapore moves towards the year 2000.[1]

*Population Control*

The growth of the population of Singapore during the major part of the period from 1819 to the outbreak of the Second World War was essentially due to the continuous inflow of people into the country.[2] After the War the flow of immigration became negligible and population increase was caused mainly by the excess of births over deaths.[3] During the pre-war period the high rate of increase of the then smaller population was matched by the vast expansion of economic activities in the country so that population problems did not exist at that time. It was the chaotic state of the country, with serious economic dislocations and food shortages, immediately after the War that led to the provision of family planning services on an organized basis. The voluntary workers assisting in the distribution of food to the starving population were convinced that feeding the hungry children would not quite solve the problem and a better method was to provide family planning services to enable parents to plan their family size according to their means. These voluntary workers, together with other individuals sympathetic to the cause of family planning, formed the Family Planning Association on 22 July 1949.[4]

Up to the end of 1965 the Association was the only organization that provided family planning services to women who wished to plan and limit their family size. The growth of the private programme run by the Association can be examined in terms of the annual number of women seeking birth control services in its clinics. In the first two months of November and December 1949, some 600 new acceptors were recruited, and in the first full year of the Association's existence in 1950 a total of 1,871 new acceptors were registered.[5] As can be seen in Table 1, the annual number rose consistently over the years, reaching 5,938 in

1959 and finally 9,845 in 1965. The pronounced drop in new acceptors in 1966 was caused by the takeover of all the clinics, except three, in January of that year by the newly-established government Family Planning and Population Board.

TABLE 1

FAMILY PLANNING ASSOCIATION NEW ACCEPTORS, 1949 — 1968

| Year | New Acceptors | Year | New Acceptors |
|------|---------------|------|---------------|
| 1949 | 600 | 1959 | 5,938 |
| 1950 | 1,871 | 1960 | 7,472 |
| 1951 | 1,880 | 1961 | 8,070 |
| 1952 | 1,787 | 1962 | 7,189 |
| 1953 | 2,302 | 1963 | 8,429 |
| 1954 | 2,966 | 1964 | 9,339 |
| 1955 | 2,850 | 1965 | 9,845 |
| 1956 | 3,772 | 1966 | 2,145 |
| 1957 | 3,820 | 1967 | 1,349 |
| 1958 | 5,280 | 1968 | 1,017 |

In many respects the Association was a pioneer organization in the field of family planning in the local and international scene. It was one of the earliest to be established in Asia and was a founder member of the International Planned Parenthood Federation in 1952. In Singapore it was for seventeen years the only agency responsible for providing the much-needed birth control services to the masses, and by October 1968 some 87,921 new acceptors had been recruited. The work of the Association was largely responsible for precipitating the decline in fertility first noted in 1958, as well as for the continuous decline up to the time when its clinics were handed over to the government in 1966. Its increasing activities over the years have created an environment conducive to the widespread acceptance of birth control ideas and practice, and hence have played a vital role in bringing about a favourable climate for the eventual introduction of a government programme.

With limited resources at its disposal, the Association found it increasingly difficult to cope with the insatiable demand for its services in the late 1950s. Beginning from 1957, the Association made numerous requests to the then Colonial Government and later to the newly-elected Government to take over the responsibility of providing clinic services.[6] Eventually, the Government agreed and established the Family Planning and Population Board on 7 January 1966. It is important to point out that the change in official policy from one of indirect

participation to one of direct provision of birth control services was en-
unciated a few weeks after the separation of Singapore from the Federation of Malaysia on 9 August 1965 when it became obvious that the
newly independent state had to survive alone without the traditional
economic hinterland. The separation brought into sharp focus the limited small land area of Singapore and the economic difficulties con-
fronting an island state devoid of any natural resources. It was therefore
clear that checking the rapid population growth was of the utmost importance in planning the social and economic development of the country. At that time, the crude birth rate was about 30 per thousand population and the annual rate of population increase was no less than 2.5
per cent.

TABLE 2

FAMILY PLANNING AND POPULATION BOARD NEW ACCEPTORS,
1966 — 79

| Year | New Acceptors | Year | New Acceptors |
|------|---------------|------|---------------|
| 1966 | 30,410 | 1973 | 19,102 |
| 1967 | 30,935 | 1974 | 18,292 |
| 1968 | 35,338 | 1975 | 16,692 |
| 1969 | 35,643 | 1976 | 17,674 |
| 1970 | 24,230 | 1977 | 16,158 |
| 1971 | 17,749 | 1978 | 15,192 |
| 1972 | 17,666 | 1979 | 15,266 |

The work and effectiveness of the government programme may be
examined in terms of the number of new acceptors recruited by the
Board. Though 1966 was essentially a year of planning and organization
for the Board, there was a steady increase in the number of new acceptors from 411 in January to 2,234 in December, with a total of 30,410
for the whole year.[7] But many of these acceptors were in fact former
patients of the Family Planning Association clinics which were taken
over by the Board. As can be seen in Table 2, the number of new
acceptors continued to increase and reached the record high of 35,643
in 1969. Thereafter, it fell sharply to 24,230 in 1970 when abortion
and sterilization were legalized. The following year saw the number
falling sharply again to 17,749. Since then the annual numbers has
oscillated between 19,100 and 15,200 without any clear upward or
downward trend.

A comparison of the figures given in Tables 1 and 2 clearly shows that the government programme was able to recruit a much higher number of new acceptors, and was thus able to accelerate the decline in fertility from 1966 onwards. This is a good example of a government programme that was responsible for accelerating the fertility decline which had in fact commenced prior to the introduction of the programme. Fertility as measured by the gross reproduction rate was reduced by 28 per cent from 2,095 to 1,500 during the five-year period 1965—70 as compared with the 29 per cent decline recorded during the nine-year period 1957—65. In the next five-year period 1971—75 fertility was reduced by 31 per cent.

In the early 1970s some adverse trends in the number of births and the crude birth became apparent; for three consecutive years from 1970 to 1972 an upsurge in both the number of births and the crude birth rate was recorded (see Table 4).[8] This upsurge was caused partly by the appearance of birth previously postponed by mothers who had earlier become acceptors for child-spacing reasons and partly by the increasing proportion of women in the reproductive ages.[9] These adverse trends caused some concern to the government which reacted swiftly to introduce a series of beyond family planning measures to check the rising number of births. These include the liberalization of the restrictive laws concerning induced abortion and voluntary sterilization, and the introduction of several incentives and disincentives aimed at promoting the two-child family.

Induced abortion and voluntary sterilization were both liberalized and legalized on 20 March 1970 with the enforcement of the Abortion Act 1969 and the Voluntary Sterilization Act 1969. Under the former Act, approval may be given to a woman to have an induced abortion performed by a registered medical practitioner in accordance with the provisions of the Act, for socioeconomic reasons.[10] On 27 December 1974 this Act was repealed and replaced by the Abortion Act 1974 which introduced the principle of abortion on demand by incorporating very liberalized rules and extremely simplified procedures governing its operation.[11] Since then abortion has been provided simply at the request of the pregnant woman with her written consent, and her medical practitioner no longer has to be satisfied that the four grounds stipulated under section 5(2) of the old Act exist. The existing Act has been designed to make the services available at the earliest possible stage of pregnancy at the lowest cost to the clinic and the lowest price to the woman requesting an abortion. The impact of the Act over the years on the number of preganancies terminated legally is shown in Table 3. The number of legal abortions increased from 1,913 in 1970 to 14,855 in 1979.

The old Sterilization Act was also replaced by the Voluntary Sterilization Act 1974 which came into force on 27 December 1974. Under the provisions of the existing Act, sterilization may be obtained at the request of the person involved and is purely a matter between the patient and a doctor approved for the purpose.[12] Sterilization is available to persons without any children and can be performed any time

TABLE 3

LEGAL ABORTIONS AND STERILIZATIONS, 1970 — 79

| Year | Abortions | Sterilizations |
|------|-----------|----------------|
| 1970 | 11,913 | 2,372 |
| 1971 | 3,407 | 3,970 |
| 1972 | 3,806 | 6,189 |
| 1973 | 5,252 | 9,338 |
| 1974 | 7,175 | 9,567 |
| 1975 | 11,105 | 9,948 |
| 1976 | 12,930 | 10,718 |
| 1977 | 13,762 | 8,587 |
| 1978 | 14,294 | 7,787 |
| 1979 | 14,855 | 7,263 |

as long as all the necessary formalities have been completed. As can be observed in Table 3, the number of sterilizations, both male and female, was greater than the number of abortions up to 1974, and from 1975 onwards the position was reversed, caused partly by the availability of abortions on demand and partly by the saturation effect on sterilizations.

Since the late 1960s a series of incentive and disincentive measures aimed at encouraging a small family size and sterilization has been introduced. These measures may be summarized as follows:

(a) paid maternity leave for four weeks before and four weeks after each confinement is now provided for the first two confinements only;[13]

(b) accouchment fee in government hospitals is fixed at an increasing amount with advancing parity;

(c) income tax relief is allowed for the first three children only;[14]

(d) couples without children and single persons in groups of two or more are now eligible to rent or purchase HDB [Housing and Development Board] flats — in the allocation of flats, equal priority is now given to families irrespective of family size, and

families with not more than three children can now sublet their
flats;

(e) in the Primary One registration exercise, children who are the
only child in their families are given greater priority and children who are the fourth or subsequent child are given low priority.[15]

Incentives designed to promote sterilization have also been built into
the above measures aimed at promoting the small family norm. Female
employees in the civil service, not normally entitled to paid maternity
leave because they already have two children, are granted paid maternity leave prescribed by their doctors if they undergo sterilization after
the delivery. Government employees are also granted seven days' unre-
corded full-pay leave for the purpose of undergoing sterilization. The
accouchment fee for patients in Classes B and C is waived if either the
husband or wife undergoes sterilization within six months of the delivery of the baby. In the school registration exercise, children who are
the first or second child of parents, one of whom has been sterilized
after the birth of the first or second child and before the age of forty, are accorded top priority in Phase Two of the registration exercise.

*Fertility and Population Growth*

Having examined the government population policies which have
been introduced in response to prevailing demographic trends and economic circumstances, we will now proceed to look at the trends in fertility level and population growth during the same period under review.
Fertility is best measured by the gross reproduction rate which is defined as the average number of female children produced by each woman
during her whole reproductive period, assuming that no woman will die
before the end of the reproductive years. The figures for the gross reproduction rate are shown in Table 4; in this table the number of births
and crude birth rate have also been included. It should be pointed out
that the crude birth rate expressed in terms of the number of births per
thousand mid-year population is not a perfect measure of fertility level
because it is distorted by the proportion of women of reproductive ages
to the total population. What this means is that a fall in the crude birth
rate need not necessarily imply a decline in the fertility level. For instance, in 1978 the crude birth rate rose by 2.8 per cent but fertility as
measured by the gross reproduction rate declined by 0.7 per cent.

After the Second World War, the number of births increased steadily
from 43,045 in 1947 to the peak of 62,495 in 1958, after which it de-
creased every year to reach 44,561 in 1969. In the next three years it
went up to reach the high of 49,678 in 1972 and then fell sharply to

39,948 in 1975, the first time below the 40,000-level after the War. In recent years the number of births followed an up-and-down path. Somewhat similar trends are experienced by the crude birth rate. Over the years the rate fell from 45.9 in 1947 to 16.6 in 1977, after which it rose slightly.

During the early post-war years, fertility remained persistently high and even increased slightly from 3.176 in 1947 to the peak of 3.234 in 1957. From 1958 fertility declined regularly up to 1971; in 1972 it increased slightly by 0.2 per cent. The decline continued in the very next year, and by 1975 the gross reproduction rate reached 1.017 which was equivalent to a net reproduction rate of less than 1.000.[16] With the present mortality level, the net reproduction rate will be 1.000 when the gross reproduction rate stands at 1.025. The rate went up to 1.036 in 1976, but fell to 0.896 in 1977, 0.890 in 1978, and 0.880 in 1979. This means that fertility has remained well below replacement level in recent years. It is worth pointing out that Singapore is the second country in Asia, the first being Japan, to have attained replacement fertility which is a pre-condition for achieving zero population growth in the future. But while Japan took about thirty years from the time of fertility decline to reach replacement fertility, Singapore took only eighteen years from 1958 to 1975.[17]

The spectacular decline in fertility in the last two decades may be attributed to a combination of factors. In the first place, the commencement of fertility decline in 1958 was triggered off by the rising age at first marriage of women and subsequently reinforced by the fall in the proportion of women ultimately married. Secondly, there was the catalytic role played by the private family planning programme which had been providing not only clinical services to the masses but also educational and motivational activities to create the general acceptance of family planning for almost ten years prior to the descent of fertility in 1958. Thirdly, from 1966 onwards the comprehensive government programme was responsible for accelerating the decline in fertility in the late 1960s. Fourthly, the legalization of induced abortion and voluntary sterilization in 1970 and their complete liberalization in December 1974 caused fertility to decline further in the 1970s. Fifthly, additional downward pressure to the fertility movement was provided by the wide range of incentive and disincentive measures most of which were introduced in the present decade.

We must not forget the interaction of cultural, social, and economic forces that came into play during the whole process of fertility decline since 1958. These are the cultural and social variables expressed in terms of modernization, higher levels of education achieved, changing attitudes towards value of children and family size, breakdown of the extended family system, and the diminishing availability of domestic help.

TABLE 4 BIRTHS, CRUDE BIRTH RATE, AND GROSS PRODUCTION RATE, 1947 – 1979

| Year | Number of Births | Crude Birth Date | Gross Reproduction Rate | Percentage Annual Change | | |
|---|---|---|---|---|---|---|
| | | | | Births | CBR | GRR |
| 1947 | 43,045 | 45.9 | 3.176 | — | — | — |
| 1948 | 44,450 | 46.3 | * | + 3.3 | + 0.9 | — |
| 1949 | 46,169 | 47.2 | * | + 3.9 | + 1.9 | — |
| 1950 | 46,371 | 45.4 | * | + 0.4 | - 3.8 | — |
| 1951 | 48,116 | 45.0 | * | + 3.8 | - 0.9 | — |
| 1952 | 51,196 | 45.4 | 3.210 | + 6.4 | + 0.9 | — |
| 1953 | 54,548 | 45.8 | * | + 6.6 | + 0.9 | — |
| 1954 | 57,029 | 45.7 | * | + 4.6 | - 0.2 | — |
| 1955 | 57,812 | 44.3 | * | + 1.4 | - 3.1 | — |
| 1956 | 60,892 | 44.4 | 3.231 | + 5.3 | + 2.3 | — |
| 1957 | 61,757 | 42.7 | 3.234 | + 1.4 | - 3.8 | + 0.1 |
| 1958 | 62,495 | 41.1 | 3.122 | + 1.2 | - 3.8 | - 3.5 |
| 1959 | 62,464 | 39.4 | 3.048 | - 0.5 | - 4.1 | - 2.4 |
| 1960 | 61,775 | 37.5 | 2.841 | - 1.1 | - 4.8 | - 6.8 |
| 1961 | 59,930 | 35.2 | 2.688 | - 3.0 | - 6.1 | - 5.4 |
| 1962 | 58,977 | 33.7 | 2.585 | - 1.6 | - 4.3 | - 3.4 |
| 1963 | 59,530 | 33.2 | 2.560 | + 0.9 | - 1.5 | - 1.0 |
| 1964 | 58,217 | 31.6 | 2.45 | - 2.2 | - 9.6 | - 4.3 |
| 1965 | 55,725 | 29.5 | 2.296 | - 4.3 | - 6.7 | - 6.3 |

TABLE 4 (Cont.)

| Year | Number of Births | Crude Birth Date | Gross Reproduction Rate | Percentage Annual Change | | |
|---|---|---|---|---|---|---|
| | | | | Births | CBR | GRR |
| 1966 | 54,680 | 28.3 | 2.095 | − 1.9 | − 4.1 | − 8.8 |
| 1967 | 50,560 | 25.6 | 1.929 | − 7.5 | − 9.5 | − 7.9 |
| 1968 | 47,241 | 23.5 | 1.704 | − 6.6 | − 8.2 | − 11.7 |
| 1969 | 44,561 | 21.8 | 1.521 | − 5.7 | − 7.2 | − 10.6 |
| 1970 | 45,934 | 22.1 | 1.500 | + 3.1 | + 1.4 | − 1.4 |
| 1971 | 47,088 | 22.3 | 1.475 | + 2.5 | + 0.9 | − 2.5 |
| 1972 | 49,678 | 23.1 | 1.478 | + 5.9 | + 3.6 | − 0.2 |
| 1973 | 48,269 | 22.1 | 1.359 | − 3.2 | − 4.5 | − 8.1 |
| 1974 | 43,268 | 19.5 | 1.143 | − 10.4 | − 11.8 | − 15.9 |
| 1975 | 39,948 | 17.8 | 1.017 | − 8.0 | − 9.2 | − 11.0 |
| 1976 | 42,783 | 18.8 | 1.036 | + 6.6 | + 5.6 | + 1.9 |
| 1977 | 38,364 | 16.6 | 0.896 | − 11.5 | − 11.7 | − 13.5 |
| 1978 | 39,441 | 16.9 | 0.890 | + 2.8 | + 1.8 | − 0.7 |
| 1979 | 40,779 | 17.3 | 0.880 | + 3.4 | + 2.4 | − 1.1 |

Fertility decline must also be viewed in terms of the impact of rapid economic development largely through industrialization leading to, among other things, a higher standard of living and greater economic participation of women in the labour force. The increased economic participation of women has the effect of encouraging some single women to postpone marriage or remain permanently unmarried as well as forcing some married women to space or terminate child-bearing in order to retain their jobs. In so far as Singapore is concerned, the role of the government in the whole complex process of fertility decline cannot be overemphasized. The determination of the present government is clearly seen in its concerted and well-orchestrated series of legislative and other measures aimed at accelerating fertility decline in an attempt to reduce the rate of population increase.

TABLE 5

ANNUAL RATE OF POPULATION GROWTH, 1947 — 79

| Period | Annual Growth Rate (%) |
|---|---|
| 1947 — 1957 | 4.4 |
| 1957 — 1970 | 2.8 |
| 1971 | 1.7 |
| 1972 | 1.8 |
| 1973 | 1.7 |
| 1974 | 1.4 |
| 1975 | 1.3 |
| 1976 | 1.4 |
| 1977 | 1.2 |
| 1978 | 1.2 |
| 1979 | 1.2 |

The rapid decline in fertility in the context of strict immigration control implies that Singapore was able to reduce the extremely high rate of population increase that was experienced in the early post-war years to a low and manageable level in recent years. Table 5 shows that the average annual rate of population increase was about 4.4 per cent during the intercensal period 1947—57, and after fertility started to decline in 1958 the rate was lowered to 2.8 per cent during the period 1957—70. Further slackening of the growth rate occurred in the 1970s which saw the rate reduced from 1.7 per cent in 1971 to the record low of 1.2 per cent in 1977. Since then the population has been growing at an annual rate of 1.2 per cent.

## Population and Labour Force Trends towards 2000

We have observed that the population policies have facilitated the attainment of replacement fertility and the reduction of the annual population increase to the low rate of 1.2 per cent in recent years. We will now proceed to examine the impact of these policies on population and labour force trends as Singapore moves towards the year 2000. This can be accomplished by projecting the population and the labour force by quinary age group for five-year intervals of time from the base year 1975 to 2000. In making this simulation exercise, it has been assumed that the population will be closed to immigration and emigration, that mortality will proceed on a downward trend, with the life expectancy at birth improving from 68.5 years in 1975 to 73.9 years in 2030 and thereafter, and that fertility will remain constant at the replacement level of 1.025 from 1975 onwards.[18] It is in fact the official aim of the present population control programme to maintain fertility at replacement level in the future.[19] The detailed results of the simulation exercise for five-year intervals from 1980 to 2000 are presented in Table 7.

It would appear that the present policy of maintaining fertility at replacement level in the future would result in the population growing

TABLE 6

GROWTH IN POPULATION AND LABOUR FORCE, 1975 – 2000

| Year | Number | Increase | Annual Growth Rate (%) |
|------|--------|----------|------------------------|
| | | Population | |
| 1975 | 2,249,900 | — | — |
| 1980 | 2,407,548 | 157,648 | 1.36 |
| 1985 | 2,593,860 | 186,312 | 1.50 |
| 1990 | 2,785,237 | 191,377 | 1.43 |
| 1995 | 2,958,694 | 173,457 | 1.22 |
| 2000 | 3,106,729 | 148,035 | 0.98 |
| | | Labour Force | |
| 1975 | 873,000 | — | — |
| 1980 | 1,043,962 | 171,000 | 3.64 |
| 1985 | 1,149,618 | 105,656 | 1.95 |
| 1990 | 1,224,563 | 74,945 | 1.27 |
| 1995 | 1,292,990 | 68,427 | 1.00 |
| 2000 | 1,350,899 | 57,909 | 0.97 |

TABLE 7 PROJECTED POPULATION BY AGE GROUP AND SEX, 1980 – 2000

| Age | 1980 | 1985 | 1990 | 1995 | 2000 |
|---|---|---|---|---|---|
| | | | Male | | |
| 0 — 4 | 112,725 | 130,223 | 136,942 | 132,408 | 124,477 |
| 5 — 9 | 117,675 | 112,342 | 129,780 | 136,477 | 131,958 |
| 10 — 14 | 119,796 | 117,510 | 112,185 | 129,598 | 136,286 |
| 15 — 19 | 143,198 | 119,544 | 117,299 | 111,983 | 129,365 |
| 20 — 24 | 147,234 | 142,725 | 119,233 | 116,994 | 111,692 |
| 25 — 29 | 124,835 | 146,631 | 142,240 | 118,828 | 116,596 |
| 30 — 34 | 101,816 | 124,249 | 145,986 | 141,614 | 118,305 |
| 35 — 39 | 65,551 | 101,103 | 123,491 | 145,096 | 140,750 |
| 40 — 44 | 66,783 | 64,719 | 100,001 | 122,293 | 143,747 |
| 45 — 49 | 55,948 | 65,280 | 63,438 | 98,261 | 120,398 |
| 50 — 54 | 50,233 | 53,643 | 62,832 | 61,268 | 95,215 |
| 55 — 59 | 39,128 | 46,847 | 50,285 | 59,163 | 57,941 |
| 60 — 64 | 30,909 | 34,844 | 42,031 | 45,417 | 53,761 |
| 65 — 69 | 24,731 | 25,540 | 29,112 | 35,470 | 38,677 |
| 70 — 74 | 14,807 | 18,338 | 19,234 | 22,236 | 27,440 |
| 75 — 79 | 7,201 | 9,764 | 12,301 | 13,110 | 15,381 |
| 80 — 84 | 2,697 | 3,835 | 5,320 | 6,847 | 7,440 |
| 85 & over | 827 | 1,123 | 1,622 | 2,327 | 3,143 |
| Total | 1,226,094 | 1,318,260 | 1,413,332 | 1,499,390 | 1,572,572 |

TABLE 7 *(Cont.)*

| Age | 1980 | 1985 | 1990 | 1995 | 2000 |
|---|---|---|---|---|---|
| | | | Female | | |
| 0 — 4 | 105,741 | 122,192 | 128,498 | 124,243 | 116,800 |
| 5 — 9 | 110,512 | 105,456 | 121,862 | 128,151 | 123,908 |
| 10 — 14 | 113,330 | 110,390 | 105,350 | 121,740 | 128,023 |
| 15 — 19 | 136,096 | 113,183 | 110,247 | 105,213 | 121,582 |
| 20 — 24 | 139,692 | 135,824 | 112,957 | 110,027 | 105,003 |
| 25 — 29 | 119,329 | 139,315 | 135,457 | 112,652 | 109,730 |
| 30 — 34 | 99,769 | 118,888 | 138,800 | 134,956 | 112,235 |
| 35 — 39 | 65,312 | 99,250 | 118,270 | 138,078 | 134,254 |
| 40 — 44 | 65,859 | 64,770 | 98,486 | 117,359 | 137,015 |
| 45 — 49 | 53,168 | 64,950 | 63,960 | 97,294 | 115,939 |
| 50 — 54 | 44,966 | 51,972 | 63,599 | 62,719 | 95,407 |
| 55 — 59 | 35,265 | 43,334 | 50,210 | 61,564 | 60,806 |
| 60 — 64 | 30,049 | 33,181 | 40,920 | 47,554 | 58,455 |
| 65 — 69 | 26,541 | 27,209 | 30,191 | 37,393 | 43,631 |
| 70 — 74 | 17,954 | 22,533 | 23,261 | 25,991 | 32,412 |
| 75 — 79 | 10,313 | 13,649 | 17,299 | 18,060 | 20,408 |
| 80 — 84 | 5,167 | 6,611 | 8,862 | 11,403 | 12,098 |
| 85 & over | 2,391 | 2,893 | 3,677 | 4,907 | 6,454 |
| Total | 1,181,454 | 1,275,600 | 1,371,905 | 1,459,304 | 1,534,157 |

Source: Saw, Population Control for Zero Growth in Singapore

from 2.25 million in 1975 to 3.11 million in 2000. Let me emphasize that our population in the year 2000 will most probably be 3.11 million, and not 4 or 5 million as has been sometimes quoted by persons without any hard facts to substantiate their statement. In the year 2000 the number of births will be 47,643 and the number of deaths will be 20,337, with a resultant natural increase of 27,306. Table 6 shows that the population increase for the five-year period 1975—80 will be 157,648, and this figure will reach the peak of 191,378 for 1985—90, and thereafter it will be reduced progressively. The average annual rate of population increase will accelerate slightly from 1.36 per cent during 1975—80 to 1.5 per cent during 1980—85, and then it will slacken during the rest of the period until the low of 0.98 per cent is reached during the last five-year period 1995—2000.

Having derived the projected population by sex and quinary age group, we can proceed to estimate the labour force for the same five-year intervals until 2000. What we have done is to apply the 1978 age-specific labour force participation rates for quinary age groups from age 10—14 to 75 and over to the projected population for five-year intervals of time from 1980 onwards.[20] Since the relevant data are available for each sex separately, the computations are carried out for males and females independently. This method of projecting the labour force necessarily implies that we are assuming that the age-specific labour force participation rates will remain constant in the future up to the year 2000. Obviously, the rates are likely to change in the future, but there is no sure way of ascertaining how these changes will occur at the various five-year intervals of time. It is, however, true to say that the projected labour force for the males will be more accurate than that for the females because the male rates will probably undergo fewer changes than the female rates. Table 8 gives the detailed figures of the projected labour force, while a summary of the results are given in the lower portion of Table 6.

According to the above method of estimation, the labour force is expected to grow from 0.87 million in 1975 to some 1.35 million in the year 2000. The increase for five-year periods will fall progressively from 171,000 during 1975—80 to 57,909 during the last five-year period. The annual growth rate of the labour force will experience a corresponding reduction, falling from 3.64 per cent to 0.97 per cent over the next twenty years. In the main this slackening in the growth of the labour force may be attributed to the deceleration in the rate of population increase and the ageing of the population.

An idea of the ageing of the population towards the year 2000 may be observed in the following figures for the population aged 60 years and over.

| Year | Persons Aged 60 & Over | % of Total Population |
|------|------------------------|-----------------------|
| 1975 | 148,600 | 6.6 |
| 1980 | 173,600 | 7.2 |
| 1985 | 192,300 | 7.4 |
| 1990 | 233,700 | 8.4 |
| 1995 | 270,700 | 9.1 |
| 2000 | 319,300 | 10.3 |

We can expect the population aged 60 and over to more than double from 148,600 in 1975 to 319,300 in 2000. In 1975 this group of old persons constituted only 6.6 per cent of the total population, and over the years the percentage will move steadily upwards to reach 10.3 per cent in 2000. A natural consequence of the ageing of the population is that the labour force will also undergo an ageing process, with an increasing proportion of workers retiring every year. The labour force aged 40 and over will rise from about 279,000 or 26.6 per cent in 1980 to some 551,000 or 40.8 per cent in the year 2000. A more detailed picture of the ageing labour force may be seen in the figures of projected labour force by age group shown in Table 8.

*Concluding Remarks*

The limited land area of our small city state, coupled with an open economy so dependent on external factors, have left our government with no alternative but to implement a comprehensive population control programme to reduce fertility to replacement level. Having achieved this target in 1975, the present population policies are geared towards the maintenance of replacement fertility in the future so as to attain zero population growth and to stabilize the population in the future. The aim of stabilizing our population at a comfortable and manageable number is to ensure that we do not reach a permanent situation of too little land and too many people. According to my calculations of the projected population beyond the period under review, the population is expected to continue to grow from 3.11 million in the year 2000 to 3.69 million in 2040 when zero population growth will be attained. In that year the number of births will be about 50,000 and so will be the number of deaths; both the crude death rate and the crude birth rate will be 13.6 per thousand mid-year population.[21]

It is obvious that if the gross reproduction rate is maintained at not the replacement level of 1.025 but at above the replacement level, the population will not only grow faster in the future but will never stabilize at all. For instance, if fertility is allowed to remain constant at 1.359 (2.7-child family) instead of 1.025 (2-child family),

TABLE 8  PROJECTED LABOUR FORCE BY AGE GROUP AND SEX, 1980 – 2000

| Age | 1980 | 1985 | 1990 | 1995 | 2000 |
|---|---|---|---|---|---|
| | | | Male | | |
| 10 — 14 | 1,797 | 1,763 | 1,683 | 1,944 | 2,044 |
| 15 — 19 | 61,718 | 51,523 | 50,556 | 48,265 | 55,756 |
| 20 — 24 | 134,277 | 130,165 | 108,740 | 106,699 | 101,863 |
| 25 — 29 | 120,591 | 141,646 | 137,404 | 114,788 | 112,632 |
| 30 — 34 | 99,983 | 122,013 | 143,358 | 139,348 | 116,412 |
| 35 — 39 | 64,502 | 99,485 | 121,515 | 142,774 | 138,498 |
| 40 — 44 | 65,381 | 63,354 | 98,201 | 120,092 | 141,160 |
| 45 — 49 | 53,934 | 62,930 | 61,154 | 94,724 | 116,064 |
| 50 — 54 | 44,908 | 47,957 | 56,172 | 54,774 | 85,122 |
| 55 — 59 | 28,642 | 34,288 | 36,809 | 43,307 | 42,413 |
| 60 — 64 | 17,000 | 19,164 | 23,117 | 24,979 | 29,569 |
| 65 — 69 | 9,571 | 9,884 | 11,266 | 13,727 | 14,968 |
| 70 — 74 | 3,702 | 4,585 | 4,809 | 5,559 | 6,440 |
| 75 & over | 1,201 | 1,649 | 2,155 | 2,496 | 2,908 |
| Total | 707,407 | 790,406 | 856,939 | 913,476 | 965,849 |

TABLE 8 *(Cont.)*

| Age | 1980 | 1985 | 1990 | 1995 | 2000 |
|---|---|---|---|---|---|
| | | | Female | | |
| 10 – 14 | 1,247 | 1,214 | 1,159 | 1,339 | 1,408 |
| 15 – 19 | 56,344 | 46,858 | 45,642 | 43,558 | 50,335 |
| 20 – 24 | 102,255 | 99,423 | 82,685 | 80,540 | 76,862 |
| 25 – 29 | 63,364 | 73,976 | 71,928 | 59,818 | 58,267 |
| 30 – 34 | 36,715 | 43,751 | 51,078 | 49,664 | 41,302 |
| 35 – 39 | 21,814 | 33,150 | 39,502 | 46,118 | 44,841 |
| 40 – 44 | 19,824 | 19,496 | 29,644 | 35,325 | 41,242 |
| 45 – 49 | 12,601 | 15,393 | 15,159 | 23,059 | 27,478 |
| 50 – 54 | 9,263 | 10,706 | 13,101 | 12,920 | 19,654 |
| 55 – 59 | 4,867 | 5,980 | 6,929 | 8,496 | 8,391 |
| 60 – 64 | 3,634 | 4,015 | 4,951 | 5,754 | 7,073 |
| 65 – 69 | 2,548 | 2,612 | 2,898 | 3,590 | 4,189 |
| 70 – 74 | 1,400 | 1,758 | 1,814 | 2,027 | 2,528 |
| 75 & over | 679 | 880 | 1,134 | 1,306 | 1,480 |
| Total | 336,555 | 359,212 | 367,624 | 373,514 | 385,050 |

the population will grow rapidly to reach 4.5 million in the year 2000 and 5.7 million in 2040, and will continue to grow indefinitely beyond this period.[22] This alternative path of higher population growth will most probably never happen in Singapore, judging from the fertility trends in recent years. On the contrary, the present population policies have achieved more than the stated aim of maintaining fertility at the replacement level of 1.025. The evidence is shown by the fall of the gross reproduction rate to 1.017 in 1975 and further down to 0.896 in 1977, 0.890 in 1978, and 0.880 in 1979.

If fertility is allowed to persist at well below replacement level in the future, the annual rate of population growth will slacken more rapidly to reach the zero position earlier than 2040, and thereafter we will experience a declining population. What we are sure is that if this happens, the population will start to decline before it reaches 3.69 million, and at a point of time earlier than the year 2040, the precise population and year depending on how low fertility will persist below the replacement level of 1.025. To forestall such a declining population from taking place in the future, it is of prime importance to review our population policies with the aim of seeking the desired equilibrium of a population control programme that is conducive to the maintenance of replacement fertility. In my opinion, the persistence of fertility well below replacement level during four years in the past, and most probably in the next few years, should be taken as a fair warning of the need to conduct a thorough review of our population policies relating to induced abortion, voluntary sterilization, and incentive and disincentive measures. It is certainly advisable to streamline and tighten some of the more liberal and permissive aspects of the laws concerning induced abortion and sterilization, apart from relaxing some of the harsher features of the incentive and disincentive measures that have already served their purpose.

# NOTES

1. For further details, see G.G. Thomson and T.E. Smith, "Singapore: Family Planning in an Urban Environment", in *The Politics of Family Planning in the Third World,* ed. T.E. Smith (London: Allen & Unwin, 1973), and Saw Swee-Hock, *Population Control for Zero Growth in Singapore* (Kuala Lumpur: Oxford University Press, 1980).
2. Saw Swee-Hock, *Singapore Population in Transition* (Philadelphia: University of Pennsylvania Press, 1970).
3. Kernial Singh Sandhu, *Indians in Malaya: Immigration and Settlement, 1786—1957* (London: Cambridge University Press, 1969), and Saw Swee-Hock, "Trends and Differentials in International Migration in Malaya", *Ekonomi* 4, no. 1 (1963).
4. Hena Sinha, "Singapore: Family Planning Association", in *Proceedings of the Seventh Conference of the International Planned Parenthood Federation* (Singapore, 1963), International Congress Series, no. 72 (Amsterdam: Excerpta Medica, 1964).
5. *First Annual Report of the Family Planning Association of Singapore, 1949—50* (Singapore: Malaya Publishing House, n.d.).
6. *Eighth Annual Report of the Family Planning Association of Singapore, 1957* (Singapore: Malaya Publishing House, n.d.).
7. *First Annual Report of the Singapore Family Planning and Population Board, 1966* (Singapore: Government Printing Office, n.d.).
8. Saw Swee-Hock, "The Rising Number of Births in Singapore since 1970", *Singapore Statistical Bulletin* 2, no. 1 (1973).
9. Saw, *Population Control for Zero Growth in Singapore.*
10. The Abortion Act 1969, No. 25 of 1969.
11. The Abortion Act 1974, No. 24 of 1974.
12. The Voluntary Sterilization Act 1974, No. 25 of 1974.
13. The Employment (Amendment) Act, 1973.
14. Income Tax (Amendment) Act, 1973.
15. *Straits Times,* 28 July 1977.
16. Saw Swee-Hock, "Singapore: Resumption of Rapid Fertility Decline in 1973", *Studies in Family Planning* 6, no. 6 (1975).
17. Irene B. Taeuber, *The Population of Japan* (Princeton: Princeton University Press, 1958).
18. For further details, see Saw, *Population Control for Zero Growth in Singapore.*
19. *Twelfth Report of the Family Planning and Population Board, 1977* (Singapore: Secura Singapore, n.d.).
20. *Report on the Labour Force Survey of Singapore, 1978* (Singapore: Ministry of Labour, n.d.).
21. Saw, *Population Control for Zero Growth in Singapore.*
22. Saw Swee-Hock, *Population Projections for Singapore, 1970—2070* (Singapore: National Statistical Commission, 1974).

# 4

## Planning the Economy for a Surprise-free Future

### Pang Eng Fong

In 1959, if a visionary had predicted that Singapore two decades later would be the richest independent city-state the world has ever known, he would have been dismissed as a dreamer. In the same year, if someone had forecast that Singapore today would be a dependent, problem-ridden port-city in a larger political unit he would have been applauded as a realistic man of uncommon vision.

Events make fools of forecasters, especially those who extrapolate without reviewing past trends and those who are too precise about the shape of things to come. History is full of turning-points not anticipated by futurologists. The development experience of Singapore in the last two decades is one example. I will review this experience before sketching one surprise-free, that is, disaster-free, scenario for the Singapore economy in the year 2000.

### Singapore's Development Experience, 1959 — 1979

#### Development Strategies

Up to the late 1950s, Singapore functioned primarily as an entrepot linking its resource-rich hinterland to the world. Trade and supporting banking, insurance, and shipping services provided its people with a standard of living much higher than that of people in its hinterland. Extremely dependent on trade, its people were outward-looking, receptive to new ideas, and responsive to changes in the region and the world. Their adaptability and skills perfected over a century of trading in an unpredictable region were put to good use when Singapore embarked on the road to industrialization.

The decision to industrialize was made soon after the present government came to power in 1959. Representing the first shift in development policy in Singapore's history, the decision was prompted by external and internal challenges. Neighbouring countries, caught in a web of post-war nationalism, were taking steps to reduce Singapore's middleman role. Domestically, unemployment was rising as entrepot activities were not able to create enough jobs for the growing influx of school-leavers into the job market. The outlook in the late 1950s was consequently grim. Industrialization was the only way out of a vicious circle of growing unemployment, labour unrest, and political turmoil.

From 1959 to 1965, development planning in Singapore was based on access to a larger domestic market.[1] This market was lost when Singapore separated from Malaysia in 1965. Its domestic market being too small, Singapore had little choice but to pursue a new strategy emphasizing the export of labour-intensive manufactures.

To this end, plans were made to attract multinational firms, the major producers of new technology. Singapore's second development strategy was exquisitely timed. Adopted at a time when the world economy was booming and multinational firms were looking for low-cost areas to assemble their products, the strategy was remarkably successful. From 1966 to 1973, Singapore experienced the fastest period of growth in its history. During this period unemployment fell sharply and large numbers of foreign managers, professionals, and unskilled workers were imported to man labour-short factories and offices. In the process, Singapore was visibly transformed. Its entrepot economy was replaced by a diversified economic structure based on manufacturing, trade, finance, and transportation activities.

The high growth years came to an end with the oil crisis in late 1973. Since then, the Singapore economy has been moving along a lower growth path. Even so, its average growth rate of 7 per cent since 1974 is much better than that of most developing countries.

During the boom years, 1966—73, productivity per worker grew by over 7 per cent a year, thanks probably to structural shifts in the economy and an energetic work force. In the post-recession period, productivity has been growing at only 3 per cent a year. The reasons for this decline are unclear. But one of its consequences is a high rate of job creation.

In mid-1979, the government, recognizing that the labour market will be increasingly overheated in the 1980s because of an expected decline in the number of new job-seekers and that Singapore cannot compete in the long run with lower-cost countries in labour-intensive manufacturing, adopted a new industrial strategy to promote high-value industries and services. One element of this strategy is a high-wage policy to discourage the expansion of unskilled jobs and tighten control over the import of unskilled workers. A second is the design of new incentives to lure high-technology firms and encourage the export of knowledge-based services. A third element of the strategy is the expansion of engineering and technical manpower ahead of demand to meet the skill needs of high-technology firms. If successful, Singapore's latest development strategy will quicken its transition to an industrial economy. By the end of the 1980s, Singapore, if it grows at 8 per cent a year, will attain a per capita income equal to that of Japan today.

*Lessons*

Favourable world development contributed to Singapore's rapid development progress, particularly in the late 1960s and early 1970s. But these developments would not have been exploited if the domestic environment had been hostile to economic growth and planning. It is instructive to identify the major factors that have enabled Singapore to capitalize on favourable world economic conditions.

Perhaps the most important factor is political and social stability. Ruled by the same political party since 1959, Singapore has enjoyed a degree of stability known to few developing countries. Its political leaders have consequently had time to develop the institutions and policies needed to promote economic growth.

A second factor contributing to Singapore's success story is its willingness to accept and learn from foreign firms. Although once a colony, Singapore, after independence, did not try, like many other ex-colonial countries, to limit the participation of foreigners in its economy. It welcomed, especially after 1965, foreign capital and technology. By maintaining an open-door policy, Singapore has been able to restructure its economy. Had it depended on local manufacturers to develop the capacity to compete successfully in foreign markets, Singapore would most probably not be a newly-industrializing country today.

Although a market economy, Singapore does not leave market forces to determine completely the allocation of resources among different economic sectors. It employs various macroeconomic instruments to guide its free enterprise system. In this respect, Singapore's planning style differs from that of Hong Kong which relies mainly on the market system to determine economic activities. For example, it offers tax and other incentives to encourage investment in industries it needs. In the 1960s, incentives were offered to labour-intensive firms. Today, incentives are designed to attract high-technology firms (e.g., petrochemicals, industrial electronics, precision engineering, aerospace, etc.) and knowledge-based service activities (e.g., computer services, architectural and engineering services, etc.).

Singapore also regulates labour—management relations to ensure industrial peace. Through the mechanism of the tripartite National Wages Council, it strongly influences the rate of money wage increases. In addition, Singapore regulates its financial system and influences, through compulsory contributions to the Central Provident Fund, the savings rate.

So far, Singapore's blend of economic freedom and government leadership has been extraordinarily successful. Regulations have not stifled initiative and economic freedom has not led to many abuses. The hard face of capitalism has been softened by government measures to ensure that most people have the basic needs of life — food, housing, jobs, and educational opportunities. Unlike some fast-growing developing countries (e.g., Brazil, Mexico), rapid growth in Singapore has not accentuated income disparities.[2]

Three main lessons can be drawn from Singapore's development experience. One is that a market system emphasizing competition and exports increases the probability of rapid growth. Second, sound fiscal and monetary policies are essential. This means reliance on domestic savings and private capital inflow rather than budget deficits and foreign aid to finance economic development. Finally, successful development requires pragmatic leaders and practical people willing to adapt to changing circumstances.

## Singapore's Economy in the Year 2000

### *Assumptions*

Projections require assumptions. I assume that in the next twenty years, the sun will not burn up and our planet will not be invaded by aliens from outer space. On a more serious level, I predict that the nature of people in Singapore will remain unchanged, that Singaporeans will remain adaptable and retain their ability to pick sensible leaders.

Most Singaporeans will continue to find the fruits of economic growth worth the effort. They will work to acquire material goods, the supply and variety of which will expand faster than their income. Only a small number of Singaporeans will consider the goal of rapid growth unappealing. They will be mostly high-income professionals. Their emphasis on creativity and personal expression will not strike a responsive chord in most Singaporeans.

In the next two decades, growing affluence will erode the work ethic in Singapore as it will in other countries like Korea, Taiwan, and Hong Kong. But its impact will not be disastrous. Since time immemorial, every generation had deplored the work habits of the next. But the work ethic is still alive and well, especially in affluent states. Over the next two decades, the lives of Singaporeans will increasingly centre around holidays and weekends. But as long as initiative and enterprise are rewarded, their capacity to respond to economic incentives will not weaken.

Singapore is a global city extremely dependent on trade, and its economic fortunes are greatly affected by world economic conditions. For its continued prosperity, Singapore needs a healthy world economy. Believers in the long-wave or Kondratieff theory of business cycles predict a downward economic trend in developed countries in the next twenty to thirty years. If they are right, the outlook for Singapore is bleak. But theirs is a mechanistic view. New technological possibilities and markets are being discovered all the time. For example, a decade ago, the microprocessor was unknown. Its development in the

1970s has created new technological possibilities, changed production methods in many industries, and spawned a widening range of consumer and industrial electronics products.

The recently concluded multilateral trade talks in Tokyo will lead to freer trade in the 1980s and beyond. World trade grew by 11 per cent a year in the decade before the oil crisis. Since then it has increased by half the amount. There is good reason to believe that the post-1973 rate will be exceeded in the future — unless of course the international economic system collapses, for example, as a result of the destruction of oil fields in Saudi Arabia.

In the last few years, political changes in Southeast Asia have been turbulent and unpredictable. Threatened by an intransigent Vietnam, the members of the Association of Southeast Asian Nations (ASEAN) have drawn closer together politically since 1975. My scenario for Singapore in the year 2000 assumes that future political developments in Southeast Asia will not be too unsettling, that there will be no violent shifts in the balance of power in the region, and that the other ASEAN nations will continue to have stable outward-looking economies.

Since 1965, Singapore has been a sovereign state. It has shown the world that it can prosper as an independent political and economic unit. Barring any catastrophe, it should continue to be an economically viable and politically independent nation in the next two decades.

*Trends*

Interdependence in the world economy has increased greatly in the last two decades. Even large countries today cannot insulate their economies from the impact of decisions made by their trading partners. As a globally-oriented port-city Singapore will benefit from the trend towards greater economic interdependence. Demand for its transportation, telecommunication, and financial services will expand rapidly in the future. While greater economic interdependence will enlarge Singapore's intermediatory role, it will also constrain the scope and effectiveness of economic policy in Singapore. Diminished control over its economy is a price Singapore must pay for the large benefits it derives from trade and foreign investment.

Another trend that has a bearing on Singapore's growth prospects in the next two decades is the growing economic importance of Pacific Basin countries. Of all regions, the Asia-Pacific area has the brightest economic outlook. The World Bank in its latest World Development Report projects that middle-income countries in East Asia and Pacific will grow by 7.6 per cent a year in the 1980s.[3] Economic prospects for the ASEAN nations are good. Because of its location, Singapore is well placed to take advantage of the strong demand for a whole range of intermediate services and capital goods that its ASEAN neighbours will generate in the future.

In the 1960s and 1970s, manufacturing played a key role in stimulating the demand for transport, communication, finance, and related services in Singapore. In the 1980s and 1990s, the growth of manufacturing in neighbouring countries will be an increasingly important factor in determining the demand for intermediate services and goods in the Singapore economy.

A trend likely to accelerate in the future is the shift in comparative advantage among countries in the manufacture of labour-intensive exports. In the 1960s and early 1970s, firms from developed countries moved their assembly operations to developing countries such as Korea, Taiwan, Hong Kong, and Singapore where labour costs were low. As their industrialization succeeds and their income expands, these developing countries are gradually losing their comparative advantage in the production of labour-intensive products to other stable, lower-cost centres. They must move up the technology ladder or lose out in the long run to lower-cost countries. Singapore's new development strategy to attract high-technology firms and encourage the export of high-value services is an explicit recognition of the continuing shift in comparative advantage among export-oriented countries.

### One Scenario for A.D. 2000

I will present only one possible scenario for the Singapore economy in the year 2000. More optimistic or pessimistic scenarios can be developed by assuming different international and national trends. I have labelled the scenario "surprise-free" in the sense that it assumes no disaster will befall Singapore in the next two decades.

*Growth Rate.* Given its considerable assets — stability, perceptive leaders, energetic workers, enterprising businessmen, a climate conducive to risk-taking, etc. — Singapore should be able to maintain a rate of growth in the 1980s at least as high as that experienced in the post-1973 period. An 8 per cent growth — over twice the rate projected for developed countries — is well within the realm of possibility. If Singapore expands by 8 per cent a year in the 1980s, it will, by 1990, have a gross domestic product (GDP) of $44 billion (in 1978 prices). Its per capita income will stand at $19,000, roughly equivalent to that of industrial countries today.

Output growth in the 1980s will come from structural change and labour force expansion. Structural change — the shift towards higher-value activities in every sector — will raise productivity gains from its recent trend rate of 3 per cent to 6—7 per cent a year in the 1970s. Labour force growth, partly from new entrants (including immigrant workers) into the job market and partly from increased female work force participation, will add 1—2 percentage points to the projected 8 per cent growth rate.

Productivity growth averaging 6—7 per cent a year for a full decade is unusual among countries. Two notable exceptions are Japan in the 1960s and Korea in the 1970s. There has only been one period on Singapore's recent economic history when its productivity grew by over 7 per cent a year. This occurred between 1966 and 1973, a period of rapid growth and structural change. If Singapore succeeds in attracting new high-value activities and in shedding some of its labour-intensive industries through a high-wage policy, a 6—7 per cent productivity growth rate is possible. One contributory factor to high productivity growth will be growing pool of skilled workers as a result of the continuing expansion of training programmes and educational opportunities.

In the 1990s, the pace of Singapore's economic growth will slacken to 6 per cent a year. A newly matured industrial economy in 1990 with a per capita income similar to that of economically advanced countries today, Singapore will find opportunities for productivity gains diminishing in the 1990s. Historically, the productivity trend rate for developed countries is about two and a half per cent a year. If Singapore's productivity advances by 4—5 per cent in the 1980s, its performance, although lower than that projected for the 1980s, would still be remarkable.

In the year 2000, Singapore will have a population of 2.8 million people, half of them in the labour force, and a GDP of $78 billion (at 1978 prices). Its per capita income of $34,000 will be similar to that of the United States in the same year, assuming that the United States grows by only about 3 per cent a year between now and the end of the century.

*Labour Force Structure and Employment.* The flow of workers into the Singapore labour market will shrink absolutely in the 1980s and 1990s, thanks to the rapid decline in fertility since the early 1960s. The fertility rate may level off in the 1980s but its effect on labour force inflow will only be felt in the late 1990s.

Employment growth will exceed any likely increase in local labour supply in the next twenty years. In consequence, the labour market can be expected to be permanently tight. A persistent state of excess demand will spawn new methods to tap and save labour. Firms will reorganize their production techniques and change their product mix to use less labour. Efforts to hire more women and part-time workers, especially students, will intensify. By the end of the century, at least half the working-age women will hold jobs outside their households, compared to two-fifths today. As pay levels rise, part-time work will become increasingly attractive to students. Long before the year 2000, part-time work will be a way of life for a large number of students.

The spread of part-time work and the increase in female work force participation rate will ease but not solve the problem of persistent shortages. A continuing inflow of foreign workers, especially those with skills, will be necessary. While the flow of foreign workers may recede in a few unusually poor years, the prospect is that by the time the next century rolls around, Singapore will have more foreign workers than it has today.

The development of industrial societies has been accompanied by the expansion of white-collar, particularly professional and managerial, jobs requiring much education and training. In most industrial nations today, there are more white-collar than blue-collar workers. Contrary to popular belief, most white-collar workers are not engaged in providing personal services. The majority in fact produce intermediate services, for example, finance, insurance, business services, or perform work in goods industries, for example, as engineers, technicians, or managers in manufacturing firms.[4]

Because it has a city-economy, Singapore's employment structure is different from that of industrial countries. White-collar workers, broadly defined as professionals, managers, technologists, sales and clerical workers, have always outnumbered blue-collar or manual workers in its economy. In the future the proportion of high-level white-collar workers — professionals, managers, and administrators — will rise steadily with the expansion of high-value service and industrial activities. By the year 2000, a quarter of the working population will be employed as professionals, technicians, managers, or administrators compared to 12 per cent today. The other 75 per cent will comprise lower-level white-collar and blue-collar workers. Although older and better educated than those today, these workers in the year 2000 will mostly be employed in semi-skilled jobs, that is, jobs that require only a short period of on-the-job training for effective performance. A Singapore society dominated by professionals, technical workers, administrators, and managers will not materialize in twenty years.

*Economic Structure.* Contrary to popular beliefs, the Singapore economy in the year 2000 will probably not be dominated by manufacturing activities. True, the manufacturing sector will continue to play a leading role in transforming Singapore's economy. But its growth rate is unlikely to be much higher than that of other sectors. The finance sector will expand, reflecting rising internal demand as well as regional and world economic growth. Transport, storage, and communication, the fastest-growing sector in the Singapore economy in the post-1973 period, will probably maintain its recent growth momentum. Trade and tourism growth will not lag far behind that of the transport or finance sector. As income rises, the demand for new public services — education, health, recreation — will grow, particularly in the 1990s as the impact of an ageing population on production and consumption patterns begins to be felt. The Singapore economy of the future will most probably be as diversified as it is today.

In contrast to sectoral shifts, intra-sectoral changes will be profound. Within the manufacturing sector, there will be a steady shift towards higher-value industries. Pressured by cost and market factors, firms will upgrade themselves by changing their product mix, technology, labour requirements, or by moving their operations to lower-wage locations. Labour-intensive industries, particularly textiles, clothing, wood, furniture, will shrink in importance. But they will not wither away completely. They have not in highly industrialized countries. It is improbable that they will fade from Singapore's industrial scene in two decades.

Singapore's manufacturing output will in future be concentrated in the petroleum, petrochemicals, electronics, aerospace, and precision engineering industries. These export-oriented industries will be largely owned by foreigners. Local firms will play essentially a supporting role. Their contribution to manufacturing output will be less than what it is today. The declining importance of local manufacturers is an inevitable outcome of Singapore's strategy to rely mainly on foreign capital, expertise, and technology for its development.

With affluence and a fast-growing industrial sector, the domestic market for intermediate inputs and final products will expand. Its importance as a source of economic growth will rise. Traditionally, the domestic market has been the preserve of local entrepreneurs. But increasingly, as it expands, it will attract foreign firms which, given their edge in management and technology over local firms, will displace many local firms. The long-term outlook for local manufacturing, in contrast to prospects for the Singapore economy, is consequently poor.

In recent years, many manufacturing firms have extended their operations to cover technical service and distribution activities. Using Singapore as a base to serve the region, they have moved into such areas as warehousing, testing, and engineering design. The involvement of manufacturing companies in technical service activities is likely to accelerate in the future as Singapore's intermediatory role expands in response to regional development.

**Concluding Remarks**

In the 1960s and 1970s, the Singapore economy was transformed. Starting out from essentially a regional base, it has been internationalized with the influx of multinational firms and the expansion of trading, transportation, and communication links with industrialized countries. In the next two decades, the region will expand rapidly and Singapore's economy will be propelled forward as much by the dynamism of the region as by growth in developed countries.

By the end of this century, Singapore will catch up in terms of per capita income with most industrialized countries. Long before the year 2000, it will have "graduated" to a developed country with all the international obligations that go with it. Singapore's "graduation" will probably be much less traumatic than presently assumed. It will, however, make economic diplomacy an increasingly important component of Singapore's foreign relations, especially with less developed countries.

With the spread of affluence and the growth of a highly-educated technocratic class in the future, there will be great changes in Singapore's social structure. New social problems will emerge. And these will be much more difficult to solve than the problem of ensuring a healthy rate of economic advance. In the past twenty years, a habit of authority, readily accepted by Singaporeans, has developed in Singapore. Whether this habit of exercising and accepting authority can accommodate new lifestyles and solve new social problems is an exciting topic that I leave to others to speculate.

## NOTES

1. The hallmark of Singapore's planning style is flexibility. Since 1959, Singapore has unveiled only one formal development plan. This was for the period 1961–64 — a period of modest economic gains. A second development plan was drawn up for the second half of the 1960s. But it was abandoned because of the unanticipated British military pullout which completely upset plan targets and priorities. Since the second plan was withdrawn, Singapore has not prepared another formal 5-year planning document. It considers the exercise of drawing up formal plans of little benefit when international economic conditions affecting its economy are changing rapidly.
2. See Department of Statistics, *Report on the Household Expenditure Survey, 1977/78,* Singapore National Printers, 1979. The report calculates that the Gini coefficient — a widely used measure of income inequality — for Singapore households has fallen from 0.40 in 1972/73 to 0.37 in 1977/78.
3. The report is summarized in Johannes Linn and Lyn Squire, "World Development Report, 1979 — Main Themes", *Finance and Development,* Vol. 16, No. 3 (September 1979), pp. 35-38, 42.
4. See Jonathan Gershuny, *After Industrial Society: The Emerging Self-Service Economy,* Macmillan Press, 1978 for an elaboration of this point. Gershuny argues persuasively that the notion that a post-industrial society is a service economy is false.

# 5

# The Relationship between Political Parties and Trade Unions in the Context of Economic Development

### Lim Chee Onn

If we had a crystal ball which could forecast the milieu in which the labour movement will find itself in the year 2000, then we would be able to draw up elaborate plans to secure for ourselves the maximum benefits that the prevailing circumstances in twenty years' time will be able to offer. Needless to say, we do not own such a gadget nor is it foreseeable that such an implement will ever be in existence. On the contrary, the many forecasting models used by economists and other social scientists have the common feature of being valid only if circumstances remain *ceteris paribus,* all other things being equal. Someone once remarked that economists try to remedy the deficiencies in their forecasts by making them frequently, and this is euphemistically known as "updating projections with the latest data". In short, frequency in forecasting is supposed to make up for accuracy. Such is the state of the art.

Notwithstanding the absence of that much sought-after crystal ball, we need to peer ahead constantly to try to make out what the situation is likely to be and make preparations to attain our goals. Let us have a look at the possible economic scene in Singapore in the year 2000.

## Singapore's Economy in the Year 2000

In the year 2000, Singapore's economy will be plugged more firmly into the global trade and economic grid. Many of our industries will be links in world production systems, manufacturing high-value parts of products for assembly elsewhere. We will also have succeeded in getting some of the sophisticated assembly work done in Singapore with the inputs produced in a host of other countries, both developed and developing ones. Consequently, our industries will have become less vulnerable to protectionistic policies.

Technologically, Singapore will have made significant progress. Our industries should be mature by then, and high-technology manufacturing processes will be the rule rather than the exception. Adaptive research and development will have been firmly established to provide a continuous stream of inputs to upgrade our industrial production.

Our workers will be as familiar with a numerically-controlled machine as with a computer terminal.

The service sector will gain in importance in our economy. Three factors will contribute to this situation. The first is the increasing application of automated production systems in industries which will require fewer people per unit output. The service sector will thus have to absorb a greater portion of the work force than it does at present. This should not pose too much of a problem because of the second factor which will come into play at that time — that is, as our people become more affluent, they seek a better quality of life for themselves. There will be greater demand for medical care, education, travel, and other leisure and recreational facilities. The accent will be on quality, diversity, and sophistication. The service sector will consequently grow to meet these demands. The third factor has to do with Singapore becoming a banking, computer soft-ware, communication, and consultancy service centre. These three factors, together with the continuation of Singapore as an important trading outlet, will lead to a greater contribution by the service sector to our economy.

By the year 2000, we hope to have successfully inculcated in our workers good work values, productivity consciousness, and an appreciation of the need for continual retraining or upgrading of skills in the course of their career. While we can expect our work force to be fairly well disciplined and technically qualified, the problem will be one of motivation. With better education and greater exposure to the ways of the world, workers in the year 2000 will have high expectations which they will probably be very articulate in voicing. The success in motivating them will depend, to a large extent, on the management of the organizations they work for. This should not pose too much of a problem if by then we have a pool of local managers who are equal to the task at hand and who are fully aware of the needs and aspirations of the workers they are in charge of.

What should the role of labour be, given this scenario put together from simple assumptions and postulates? The answer lies in understanding what workers expect in return for their contributions.

Our per capita gross domestic product (GDP) by the year 2000 should be slightly higher than that which exists in Japan today. Given the size of our labour force, the only way to achieve the GDP necessary to attain this level of per capita income is to continually increase our productivity. Among the factors which can contribute towards productivity increase, the following three listed have been cited most frequently: (1) high levels of investment and increases in the capital-to-labour ratio; (2) significant advances in technology and its application in industrial production; and (3) rapid growth of the global economy and trade, leading to larger export markets and the attendant benefits through economies of scale in production.

There is a fourth factor which is of direct concern to trade unions. This is the state of the industrial relations environment, particularly the incidence of labour disputes and work stoppages. So far we have managed to maintain a fairly healthy industrial relations environment which partly accounts for our relatively painless passage through the recession of the last few years. We will have to sustain such a situation over the next two decades. In this respect, unions on their own can achieve little unless they have the full cooperation of managements and the Government.

Joint consultation between labour and management is critical in this matter, and will probably have become an established feature in our industrial relations system. It is conceivable that by then this relationship will have become institutionalized on a tripartite basis where formal consultations on industrial relations matters take place regularly instead of on an *ad hoc* basis.

Closely allied to this will be the concerted effort directed at further improving the quality of working life. As indicated earlier, we shall be dealing with educated and skilled workers who have definite ideas of what they want and expect, from employers as well as unions. Greater democratization of the work place can be expected, with more delegation of responsibility and authority down the line. Unions will have to ensure that shopfloor leaders on their part are sufficiently skilled, mature, reliable, and knowledgeable to take on this role. Branch unionists will be specialists in their respective fields to provide the necessary support. Training programmes to meet this need will have become a common feature of union activities.

Norms for excellence in production quality and reliability for various industries will have been established. Each of our workers will be expected to be his own quality controller and zero-defect standards will be the norm rather than the exception. In return, workers can look forward to good wages and even higher living standards.

Unions will have to meet some of the leisure-oriented needs of the workers. The general work force will guard their leisure more jealously. This is a healthy development as long as such leisure is faithfully earned and usefully spent. By then, the union as a social organization will have taken root. Meeting the leisure needs of our workers will be a natural extension of the union's social role.

Wage earners generally are concerned about inflation. One of the main roles of the labour movement will be to help contain inflation brought about by higher cost of energy, a high consumption society, a tight labour market, and possibly an imbalance between the supply and demand of goods and services. One such measure is for our union cooperative network to expand and act as a price leader for essential commodities and services, thereby helping to curb profiteering. This will be supplemented by efforts to help the Government set up some form of price-monitoring machinery, either through legislation and enforcement or through the strengthening of our Consumer Association (CASE) which should have a well-established claims court by then.

The industrial scene in the year 2000 which I have just outlined undoubtedly presents our workers with many opportunities. How shall we strive to get the most out of them? At our recent seminar on "Progress into the Eighties" and the NTUC [National Trades Union Congress] Triennial Delegates Conference, unionists have debated at length on the preparations which workers and unions ought to make to secure for themselves the best the future can offer. Today I propose to examine in slightly greater detail one of the facets of the union movement which was touched on during the conference. I shall talk about the relationship between the political party in power on the one hand and trade unions on the other, and the effect this relationship has on national development and economic progress.

## Party—Union Relationship

While a time-series forecast is generally fraught with uncertainty, a cross-country comparison properly applied can bring many benefits. In other words, a study of how others have made it to the level which we hope to attain can give us some idea of the preparations that are required, the pitfalls that will be encountered, and the implications of the available options. I therefore propose to examine very briefly the political party—trade union relationships in Britain and Germany, and draw some conclusions from their experiences. Given the structure of our political system, the level of our national income, the nature of our economy, and the history of our trade union movement, I think it is worthwhile to study these two models. There are of course experiences of other countries which we can also learn from, notably Japan and Sweden, but time precludes such exhaustive comparisons on this occasion.

One of the great difficulties encountered in the matter of unions and government policy, as generations of legislators have found, is to determine the "legitimate" scope for union activity. Only totalitarian governments deny trade unions the basic right to organize and to engage in collective bargaining. However, in the democracies it has proved difficult to decide whether the state should adopt a neutral or biased stance towards trade unions. The great variety of legislation concerning the rights of unions in industrial relations matters in different countries indicates the extent of this dilemma.

In some countries, governments have adopted a pro-union stance, particularly Britain in the last few years prior to the return of the Conservatives to power. This is most obvious in the very extensive rights and immunities which unions enjoy within the law to extend their organizations, establish closed-shops, and engage in picketing and secondary boycotts. In other countries such as Japan and West Germany, governments have adopted a more neutral stance towards unions and have limited their rights within the law to a far greater extent than in Britain.

None the less, in Britain and West Germany, like in many other countries, trade unions and their confederations pursue their key objectives through long-established links with political parties. At the same time, most political parties take into account the aims of trade unions when formulating their programmes and objectives, even if they lack formal links to the unions. There is hardly any alternative.

Political parties aspiring or clinging to power can no more afford to disregard the vital concerns of major trade union groups than trade unions can afford to abstain from participation in the political process. If there is a choice, it is not over the principles of party—union interaction but over degrees of commitments, and over subtle but important distinctions between what is justifiable and what is excessive influence.

It is clear that it is not the overt intention of any of the democratic governments to bring about a situation in which the influence of trade unions is total and absolute. A simple illustration will show why this has to be so. In a situation when the power of unions is absolute, the wage level and wage structure, for example, will be determined totally by unions and the labour market will be constrained to function by a system of non-price rationing which can have potentially disastrous consequences for the economy. Obviously this is not desirable from any point of view.

## The Experience of the British Trade Union Congress

Britain is seen to be closer to this sort of situation than any other Western economy. The reasons for this are complex. The history and development of the British trade union movement is distinctive and has produced an unusual pattern of party—union relations in which the British Labour Party is the direct agency of its political expression. Thus, the structure, procedures, and financial base of the Labour Party indicate a degree of integration with and dependence on the trade unions that places the party—union relationship in a unique category. Table 1 showing the distribution of votes within the British Trade Union Congress and the Labour Party Conference illustrates this very clearly. About 88 per cent of the total number of votes at the Labour Party Conference was cast by unions. The figures are for 1973, but the pattern has not changed much since then.

For the British trade unions, this historical relationship gives them the reassurance that their fundamental industrial interests will be protected and that the party will in general help them to realize their long-term economic and social aspirations. For the party's parliamentary leadership, the link with the organized working class is an electoral asset, not only in the financial resources available from the unions for fighting elections but also in the base of electoral support it can muster.

Such a relationship, one would have thought, augurs well for party, unions, and the nation. However, the political influence of unions, apart from being a nation's strength, can also be the cause of its decline. It is hardly controversial to assert that the British trade union movement has exerted considerable influence on the policies pursued by the Labour Government and, to some extent, on the Conservative Government.

For the most part, Conservative Governments have recognized in the trade union movement a powerful adversary and have, at various times, accommodated the unions on a number of issues but more generally have tried to avoid conflict with them. In contrast, Labour Governments have effectively been drawn into a political alliance with the unions and have promoted policies designed to further the political aspirations of the unions. What went wrong was the application by the unions of such formidable political influence in the wrong direction. Let me illustrate this through two examples — the nationalization of industries and the provision of unemployment benefits.

Unions are most effective in gaining their wage objectives where they are dealing with state monopolies which are largely free from the discipline of competition. It is also in state-owned corporations that successive British governments have demonstrated their willingness to provide an apparently inexhaustible supply of finance to avoid the collapse of the industry or, more recently, even any significant adverse economic consequences for the labour force. In such situations the unions are largely freed from the constraints of consequential unemployment normally associated with an aggressive wage policy. British Steel, British Shipbuilders, and Rolls Royce are examples of monopolies which have been taken into state ownership, largely at the behest of the trade unions. All three persistently make losses, yet they are among the firms in the country paying the highest wages, where aggressive trade union policies are being pursued with little fear of resultant job losses.

Unions operating in this environment of state-owned monopolies are not, in any real sense, engaged in an economic struggle with capital, nor are they operating against the background of the usual market rules. Instead they are often thought to be engaged in extracting from the public purse as much as they can in the knowledge that redundancies are a remote prospect, and that losses as a result of their activities

TABLE 1

DISTRIBUTION OF VOTES WITHIN THE BRITISH TRADE UNION
CONGRESS AND THE BRITISH LABOUR PARTY
CONFERENCE 1973

| Trade Union Congress | Number of Votes | Labour Party Conference | Number of Votes |
|---|---|---|---|
| Two largest unions | | Two largest unions | |
|   Transport workers | 1,747,000 | Transport workers | 1,074,000 |
|   Engineers | 1,342,000 | Engineers | 897,000 |
|   Total | 3,089,000 | Total | 1,971,000 |
| Ten largest unions | 6,451,000 | Ten largest unions | 4,213,000 |
| Total votes cast by all unions represented at the Congress (97 organizations) | 9,742,000 | Total votes cast by all unions represented at the Conference (56 organizations) | 5,449,000 |
| | | Total votes cast by all Constituency Labour Parties represented at the Conference | 702,000 |
| | | Total votes cast by all Socialist, Co-operative, and Professional organizations represented at the Conference (15 organizations) | 46,000 |
| | | Total Conference vote | 6,197,000 |

Source: Lenis Minkin, "The British Labour Party and the Trade Unions: Crisis and Compact", *Industrial Labour Relations Review* 28, no. 1 (Oct. 1974): 23.

will be made good by way of subsidies. It is therefore not hard to see why unions are among the leading advocates of the nationalization of industry in Britain.

Those who pay the price for the economic gains made by the unions in nationalized industries are consumers, the economically inactive, and the taxpayers. This is obviously untenable. Moreover, since many of the nationalized industries persistently lose money because they are not commercially viable, sustaining these enterprises will result in resource misallocation which imposes a cost on the whole community.

However, none of these reasons is intended to be an argument against the principle of state ownership of industry. Instead they are arguments against the nationalization of any industry for the purpose of placating the desire of unions for a favourable environment in which to pursue their sectional objectives at the expense of the rest of the community.

This serves to illustrate that misplaced power of the unions can result in their extracting more and more from the consumer and the public purse without paying heed to the economic and social implications of their activities.

Next we come to the subject of unemployment benefits, a matter which is much talked about and sometimes admired, at least by the slothful. It is hard to see how any society can justify a system of unemployment compensation that encourages people to prefer unemployment to work, and that pays to the unemployed more than what a substantial proportion of the work force can earn in work. Quite apart from the perceived "unfairness" of such a system, it also brings about serious consequences for the growth potential of the economy. Nor is a system of this nature likely to be an efficient way of achieving its ostensible social objective of shielding the unemployed from poverty. An economic rationale for the system that has occasionally been advanced is that it permits workers who are laid off to search for new employment more effectively. There has been no evidence that this has been the case.

The ambivalence which is associated with high unemployment benefits is due to the continual demands from the trade unions for the government to reduce the unemployment level, while advocating the increase in unemployment benefits which are partly to blame for the high level of unemployment in the first place. A system which chases its own tail gets exhausted very quickly. Total collapse follows not far behind. Lubrication from North Sea oil does help to keep the system going for a little while longer.

The moral of these two examples is that if unions pursue their objectives blindly, success is achieved only at substantial cost to the community as a whole.

*The Experience of the West German Trade Union Confederation*

The party—union relationship in the Federal Republic of Germany (FRG) has produced results different from those found in Britain. The most important consequence of this relationship in West Germany has been the moderating influence it has exerted on both major political camps.

In the Socialist Party, the union elements have used their weight to support gradualist and pragmatic reform policies and to oppose effectively the more extreme proposals of the Young Socialists and the New Left. Among the Christian Democratic groups, the trade unionists have pushed their party into adopting a more centrist approach to controversial social policy issues than what the conservative on the right of the party espouse.

It is therefore not surprising that among the economic interest groups in West Germany, the German Trade Union Confederation, the DGB, has been politically pre-eminent in the spheres of labour, social, and economic policy at the national level. This is not to say that national policy in these areas always reflects the undiluted wishes of the DGB, only that, in recent years, compromises put together by party and government leaders usually give a slight edge to its position.

One fundamental determinant of union influence in West Germany has been a general attitude of political corporatism, an attitude inherited from medieval times in Europe. Corporatism leads German politicians to believe that the interest of all the various major groups in West Germany must be taken into account and balanced in the determination of public policy. The first inclination of policy-makers is thus to seek out group representatives to discover their views and then determine how their various interests can best be balanced. The notion of balance is important. A "winner-take-all" attitude is not a part of corporatism, and indeed such an attitude seldom benefits any of the parties in the long run as the British unions are finding out to their chagrin.

In a corporatist system, the question becomes, "which group will decision-makers seek out to speak for a particular interest?" The founders of the DGB created a leading position for their organization as the post-war spokesman for labour by largely overcoming the structural weaknesses in the labour movement of the Weimar period. At that time, organized labour was divided into a number of different political alignments, including Socialist, Christian, Liberal, and Communist. In 1931, membership of these parties as a percentage of organized employees was 55 per cent, 15 per cent, 7 per cent, and 4 per cent respectively. Only about 19 per cent of organized workers were in associations not aligned with any particular party. Within some of the alignments, additional divisions resulted from the three different occupational classes in German life, namely, industrial workers, white-collar employees, and civil servants. This structure was held to be a cause of political weakness during the Weimar period, especially fateful in that the labour movement could do little to check the rise of Nazism.

To overcome such a discrete structure, union leaders from various alignments who survived the Nazi period resolved to form a united trade union that would encompass all organized labour in a single union. This conception was diluted somewhat when the DGB came into being in 1949 as a confederation of sixteen industrial unions.

The enormous DGB membership, towering over that of any other organization in the Federal Republic, enables the confederation and its constituent unions to recruit sizeable staffs of technical experts on various labour, social, and economic matters. Political decision-makers give weight to organized groups not only because of corporatist notions but also because they have found that the technical expertise of these groups is useful in drafting and administering policy. The capacity of the West German unions to provide technical expertise further helps to explain their political influence. I feel that this is a worthwhile position for our unions to work towards so that we can truly become equal partners with the party in development.

An overshadowing fact of political life for the DGB has been its close relationship with the Social Democratic Party (SPD). The spirit of this relationship is well captured in the words of Walter Freitag, president of the DGB, to the annual convention of the SPD in 1954:

> I have the mandate to convey to your party convention the best wishes and greetings of the executive board of the Deutscher Gewerkschaftsbund (DGB). I do this all the more gladly because I know I am among people who are most intimately bound up with us, the German trade union movement. A division between the Social Democratic Party and the German trade unions is inconceivable. We are the children of one mother. . . .

What political meaning did this extensive relationship have? Certainly it did not mean that in any way the DGB controlled party policymaking. It did mean, however, that the party in its decision-making was well acquainted with union views. Moreover, in corporatist fashion, and given a need for technical expertise, the party took special note of union views in those spheres seen as most intimately the concern of the unions. Conversely, party views were well represented in union decision-making. In fact, the more accurate picture is not so much one of party views and union views separately formulated and then accommodated, but of continual mutual shaping of views into similar positions. There is much to be said for such a decision-making process.

In practical politics, the trade unions contribute to the SPD in four areas: membership recruitment, voting support, propaganda support, and indirect financial aid. The first area is the most important.

Since the unions have so many more members and officials than the party, it may be assumed that many more party members are recruited from the unions than union members from the party, although the latter type of recruitment does take place. Some evidence for this assumption is provided by the biographies of members of the 1969 Bundestag. Of forty-four members of the SPD Fraktion who had at one time or another held an official function in the unions, sixteen were either union members or officials before joining the SPD or taking on an official function in the party, seven became party members first, and three joined both party and union in the same year. The remaining eighteen members' background was unclear. Recruitment is an important service for the party since the SPD is fairly dependent financially on the dues and contributions of its mass membership.

Generally, in the post-war period, German union leaders have played a statesman's role in the sphere of collective bargaining. As a result of a strong demand for goods and a tight labour market since the mid-1950s, the unions have normally held the strongest hand in bargaining. A generally acknowledged part of the West German economic miracle, however, has been the readiness of union leaders to take a long-term view of the impact of economic policies on their members' welfare. A good example was their decision to hold back their wage demands sufficiently to prevent too great an inflation of costs when they could have easily gone through with their demand during the tight labour situation. In 1967, the participation of the unions in a kind of macro-economic planning was institutionalized when the SPD Minister for Economic Affairs set up a working group called Concerted Action. Meeting several times each year, representatives of government, industry, labour, and agriculture worked together voluntarily to maintain a healthy economy. This close cooperation eventually led to the strong German economy of today.

These two brief outlines on the British and German experiences on party—union relationship show that political parties with a primary working class base recognize the advantages of expanding their electoral appeal through trade unions. For their part, unions recognize the benefits of an association with a fraternal party, and it is up to them to make the best use of such links to further the interest of workers and their members. What lessons can our trade unions draw from these experiences as we ponder over our role for the twenty-first century?

## Lessons for NTUC

The success Singapore has enjoyed in attracting foreign investments was due, among other favourable factors, to the quality of its labour force, the harmonious industrial relations environment, and most important of all the unions' relationship with the ruling party. It was enlightened self-interest that largely determined the unions' response to governmental policies, and this symbiotic relationship between the party and the unions contributed significantly to our achievements.

The question of wages is one good example. Wage policies have been carefully formulated and implemented, both to dampen the effects of inflation on workers and to encourage investors and domestic savings. At the same time, every effort was made to ensure that benefits from higher productivity and profits are equitably shared among those who have contributed. This has led to a steady rise in the standard of living of workers without creating the feast or famine situation, sometimes known as a stop-go economy, prevalent in some economies.

The experiences of the British and German unions have illustrated vividly what can and cannot be achieved; and what the long-term benefits are, given clear-headed thinking and the will to implement necessary but unpopular policies. Obviously, circumstances vary from country to country, each with its own history, tradition, and set of priorities. I do not propose to run through the development of the party—union relationship between the People's Action Party (PAP) and the National Trades Union Congress (NTUC). The history of the PAP and our labour movement has been fairly well documented and, I suspect, most people will already have at least a broad understanding and grasp of the roles of these two organizations in their contributions to the development of Singapore.

What I propose to do now is to make certain inferences about union activities and their impact on economic development. I shall be the first to admit that the treatment that follows is far from being rigorous, and purists will probably flinch at the approach. None the less I feel that it will be useful for us to get at least a feel of the parameters and preconditions for continued growth.

Table 2 shows the trade union membership in the FRG, the United Kingdom, and Singapore. I have also included Japan's figures for comparison among the industrialized countries. The table sets out trade union density for each of the four countries, that is, union membership as a proportion of the employed labour force, with separate figures for three sectors of employment — private blue-collar employment, private white-collar employment, and public employment. Unfortunately, more up-to-date figures are not available. They none the less confirm that the public sector generally has a higher percentage of organized workers for the reasons I gave while discussing nationalized industries.

TABLE 2

TRADE UNION MEMBERSHIP IN FOUR SELECTED COUNTRIES

| Country | Overall % | Private Employment | | Public Employment % |
|---|---|---|---|---|
| | | Blue-Collar % | White-Collar % | |
| Federal Republic of Germany (1972) | 37[a] | 42 | 19 | 93 |
| United Kingdom (1973) | 50[a] | 50 | 27 | 85 |
| Singapore (1978) | 32[b] | 36 | 17 | 56 |
| Japan (1977) | 33[b] | 29[c] | | 62 |

Source: *This is Sohyo — Japanese Workers and Their Struggles* (Sohyo, Japan, 1978), p.1.

*Report on the Labour Force Survey of Singapore,* 1978.

Notes:  a = % of Total Employed Labour Force
   b = % of Organizable Work Force
   c = Average of total private sector

The trade union membership as a percentage of labour force does not vary significantly among the four countries. However, a study of the industrial disputes in terms of working days lost reveals a marked difference. Table 3 shows this very clearly. The figures for the number of man-days lost per thousand employed persons are a fair comparison since the labour force employed differs among the four countries. The trend over the period 1968–77 is significant. Both West Germany and Japan show a downward trend in the number of working days lost per thousand employed persons, while Britain shows a sustained high figure. I do not think that this difference can be attributed solely to the fact that British managers are more recalcitrant or less sensitive to workers' motivation than their counterparts elsewhere. I think that every country has its fair share of unenlightened employers. The answer may lie in unions' attitudes.

We then come to the whole purpose of work, namely, the production of goods and services. Table 4 shows the growth of real gross national product (GNP) of the four countries. The FRG and Japan show consistently higher growth rates than the United Kingdom. It will be invidious to infer anything from Tables 3 and 4 by trying to establish a relationship between the economic growth of a country and its prevailing state of industrial relations, as there are many factors that determine the rate of increase of national output. However, I feel that these figures do indicate something, inconclusive though it may be. I leave it to you to draw your own conclusions, but on the surface there appears to be some link between the average rate of GNP growth and the trend of industrial disputes over the same period.

Similarly, another set of figures showing wage-rate increases and productivity growth gives some indication of wage policies prevailing in the country. If wages increase at a rate which is higher than, and out of step with, productivity increase, this will have a tremendous impact on production costs and competitive edge of exports. This impact in turn could well affect the real growth of the GNP and wage increase for workers. Tables 5 and 6 show the wage indexes and rates of productivity growth respectively for West Germany, the United Kingdom, and Japan. While I hesitate to conclude anything from a set of isolated figures, I am tempted to say that the higher productivity growths for West Germany and Japan have enabled their wage rates to increase relative to Britain's without affecting the competitiveness of their exports.

In any study on industrial relations, West Germany generally is held up as the exemplar in adopting an enlightened approach in striking a balance between pursuits of trade union objectives and national interest. In fact, in nearly all instances, the DGB has perceived that the interest of the workers and that of the nation converge, for after all, unionized workers make up a large part of the citizenry. Tables 2 to 6, to some extent, illustrate this philosophy of the DGB and its consequences.

What the study of the British and West German experiences in party—union relationship has shown is that there are many reasons how such a relationship has come about. It was partly history, partly the vision of a number of political and trade union leaders, and partly circumstances of the day. In Singapore, the development of the relationship between the political party (PAP) and the trade unions (NTUC) has fairly similar beginnings, and the link was nurtured and strengthened by the strive for national survival. The issue to which we now have to address ourselves is how to capitalize on this relationship for the benefit of our workers.

The lesson to draw from the experiences of the British and West German unions is that it is imperative for unions to reconcile the needs

TABLE 3    INDUSTRIAL DISPUTE COMPARISON FOR FOUR COUNTRIES

| Country | Code | 1968 | 1970 | 1972 | 1974 | 1976 | 1977 |
|---|---|---|---|---|---|---|---|
| Federal Republic of Germany | A | — | 129 | 54 | 890 | 1,481 | 81 |
| | B | 25,167 | 184,269 | 22,908 | 250,352 | 169,312 | 34,437 |
| | C | 25,249 | 93,203 | 66,045 | 1,051,290 | 533,696 | 23,681 |
| | D | 25,491,000 | 26,169,000 | 26,125,000 | 25,688,000 | 24,556,000 | 24,488,000 |
| | E | 1.0 | 3.6 | 2.5 | 40.9 | 21.7 | 1.0 |
| United Kingdom | A | 2,378 | 3,906 | 2,497 | 2,922 | 2,016 | 2,703 |
| | B | 2,257,600 | 1,800,700 | 1,734,400 | 1,626,400 | 668,000 | 1,165,800 |
| | C | 4,690,000 | 10,980,000 | 23,909,000 | 14,750,000 | 3,284,000 | 10,143,000 |
| | D | 24,436,000 | 24,373,000 | 24,019,000 | 24,715,000 | 24,425,000 | 24,547,000 |
| | E | 191.9 | 450.5 | 995.4 | 596.8 | 134.5 | 413.2 |
| Singapore | A | 4 | 5 | 10 | 10 | 4 | 1 |
| | B | 172 | 1,749 | 3,168 | 1,901 | 1,576 | 406 |
| | C | 66.6 | 1.4 | 5.8 | 2.8 | 2.0 | 2.5 |
| | D | 580,000 | 651,000 | 725,000 | 803,000 | 845,000 | 883,000 |
| | E | 0.12 | 0.002 | 0.008 | 0.004 | 0.002 | 0.003 |
| Japan | A | 1,546 | 2,260 | 2,498 | 5,211 | 2,720 | 1,712 |
| | B | 1,163,357 | 1,720,135 | 1,543,557 | 3,621,049 | 1,356,025 | 691,908 |
| | C | 2,840,866 | 3,914,807 | 5,146,668 | 9,662,945 | 3,253,715 | 1,518,476 |
| | D | 50,020,000 | 50,940,000 | 51,260,000 | 52,370,000 | 52,710,000 | 53,420,000 |
| | E | 56.8 | 76.9 | 100.4 | 184.5 | 61.7 | 28.4 |

A = Number of disputes
B = Workers involved
C = Working days lost
D = Labour force employed
E = Number of working days
    lost per thousand
    enployed persons

Source: *Labour Disputes Statistics*, Ministry of Labour, Japan
        *Year Book of Labour Statistics*, International Labour Office
        *Wirtschaft und Statistik*, Bureau of Statistics, FRG
        *Department of Employment Gazette*, Department of Employ-
        ment, UK

Notes:  Japan       –  Exclude workers indirectly affected and disputes
                        lasting less than 4 hours.

        FRG         –  Exclude disputes lasting less than 1 day except
                        when a loss of more than 100 working days is
                        involved.

        United      –  Exclude disputes not connected with terms of
        Kingdom        employment or conditions of labour. Disputes
                        involving less than 10 workers or lasting less than
                        1 day are not included unless a loss of more than
                        100 working days is involved.

of its members with national interest. If a union's prime interest is to protect and improve the living standards of its members, does this mean that this is achievable only if national interest is to take second place? The German DGB has shown clearly and conclusively that this need not be so.

On the other hand, looking at the British experience, one gets the impression that a party—union relationship has to be one of a battle for power between two groups with apparently conflicting interests. Trade unionism is the collective activity of wage earners in protecting and improving the conditions of their working lives. The Government on its part is the custodian of anything and everything which affects the national interest. Who should then call the tune? This, of course, brings us to the question of what is in the national interest. Is national interest anything the Government thinks is important at a particular time irrespective of what it is?

In a democratic freely-elected government, the answer to this question must be in the affirmative since the government derives its authority and mandate from the people. It is therefore unavoidable that union action has to be tempered and limited by the values of the system society upholds and prefers. Does this mean that unions consequently

TABLE 4

GROWTH OF REAL GROSS NATIONAL PRODUCT/
GROSS DOMESTIC PRODUCT IN FOUR COUNTRIES

| Country | Average 1965/66 to 1975/76 | Growth Over Previous Year | | |
|---|---|---|---|---|
| | | 1977 | 1978 | 1979 (June) |
| Federal Republic of Germany[a] | 3.3 | 2.6 | 3.4 | 3.75 |
| United Kingdom[b] | 2.1 | 2.0 | 3.2 | 1.25 |
| Singapore[c] | 10.7[d] | 8.1 | 8.6 | 9.7 |
| Japan[a] | 8.2 | 5.4 | 5.6 | 5.5 |

Source: *OECD Economic Outlook,* no. 25 (July 1979), p. 17.
        *Year book of Statistics,* Department of Statistics, Singapore, 1978/79, p. 3.

Notes:  a =  Gross National Product in 1965 Prices
        b =  Gross Domestic Product in 1965 Prices
        c =  Gross Domestic Product in 1968 Prices
        d =  Average GDP for period 1968—76

TABLE 5

COMPARISON OF PER-HOUR WAGE INDEXES, 1955 AND 1977

(A) 1955

| Federal Republic of Germany | United Kingdom | Japan |
|---|---|---|
| 100 | 268 | 50 |

(B) 1977

| Federal Republic of Germany | United Kingdom | Japan |
|---|---|---|
| 100 | 52 | 86 |

Sources:   Japan — *Monthly Labour Survey,* Ministry of Labour
Other countries — *Yearbook of Labour Statistics,* ILO.
             *Department of Employment Gazette* (U.K.)

Notes:   (1)   Indexes are based on wages of production workers in manu-
              facturing.
         (2)   Exchange rates: 1955 — US$ = Y 360 and DM4.2; 1978 —
              US$1 = Y221 and DM2.1.
         (3)   Japanese wages are the total cash earnings which include
              bonuses.

become ineffective and inadequate in fulfilling their roles for which they have been set up to perform? The German experience has shown otherwise. On the contrary, the DGB has become that much stronger as a result of promoting the national interest.

German trade unions have shown that finding a common bond with the party or government and working together for the prosperity of the nation benefits everyone. The experience of striving together bred a comradeship, a commitment on both sides to work for the common good. The success of the German economy and the prosperity of the German worker demonstrate clearly that people delude themselves if they imagine that progress can ever take place without effort. Unfortunately, some still seem to believe that there can be stability without a strong and honest government, enterprise without entrepreneurs, riches without savings, jobs without profits, higher output without effort, and a better standard of living without initial sacrifice. Those who harbour such illusions will be well advised to re-think their policies.

While it has been helpful to look at the experience of Britain and West Germany to see what can be learnt and adapted to our own situation, wholesale transplant, as in heart surgery, is likely to produce rejection. However, one lesson is clearly demonstrated. Political party— trade union relationship determines to a large extent the direction

TABLE 6

AVERAGE ANNUAL RATES OF PRODUCTIVITY
GROWTH IN FOUR COUNTRIES, 1963–73 AND 1973–77

| Country | Productivity Growth | |
| --- | --- | --- |
| | 1963–73 | 1973–77 |
| Japan | 8.7 | 2.8 |
| Germany | 4.6 | 3.2 |
| United Kingdom | 3.0 | 0.5 |
| Singapore | – | 3.1[a] |

Source: *OECD Economic Outlook,* no. 25 (July 1979), p. 29.
*Report on the Labour Force Survey of Singapore,* 1973–78, Research
and Statistics Division, Ministry of Labour, Singapore.
Note:    a =   Average Annual Growth of Real Value-Added per Worker 1973–78.

of national development. It can either progress or regress. The choice is
up to the two parties in the relationship. I think the choice is clear for
the NTUC if we want to prepare our members adequately to meet the
challenges in the year 2000.

Individually and collectively, the NTUC is committed to Singapore
— to its stability, security, and progress. We place human dignity above
all else, and this will be the basis on which our principles and policies
are formulated. So does the political leadership of our nation, which
governs on the basis of overwhelming electoral endorsement.

The earlier roles of our unions — as the vehicle for our anti-colonial
government struggle, as a class movement, or as a militant revolutionary
force — have been largely replaced by one of a contributor to and co-
owner of our society. A mutually responsible cooperation between the
party and political leadership on the one hand, and the trade unions on
the other, has been the history of modern Singapore. It will be a mistake to assume that because the unions stood solidly with the party
they have forfeited their independence or weakened their function as
trade unions. Our workers' prosperity today bears testimony to the
success of such a relationship. This relationship will have to continue
and to be strengthened if we wish to reach greater heights of achievement and prosperity for our workers and people in the twenty-first
century.

# 6

## Images of Man-made Environment

Liu Thai Ker

When we think about life in the year 2000, we tend to conjure up fantastic images of revolutionary transportation systems and entirely new arrays of gadgets and robots. This seems to be reasonable as twenty years is a long time in this rapidly changing era. However, if we look backwards over twenty years or draw upon the experiences of other developed countries, it is in fact not easy to make big changes in two decades. Basic human needs do not run wild like fantasies, and new technology must fulfil some real needs at economical prices if it is to gain wide acceptance. For example, there have been various floating-city schemes. As far as we know, none has materialized yet although much engineering ingenuity has been exercised in the past twenty years.

Therefore, in the next two decades we still have to do much the same things that we have been doing over the last twenty years. The city as a whole still has the arduous task of squatter and slum clearance, pollution control, infrastructure upgrading, etc. Whereas today many urban areas are steadily deteriorating, we can be reasonably sure that ours will become cleaner and more livable. The visual images will become more orderly and beautiful. Buildings will improve in design and construction, more in pace with the latest innovations than it was in the past, but unlikely to depart drastically from the current essentially rectangular, post and beam structures, mostly high-rise. This would seem to be the general picture of the man-made environment in Singapore in the next two decades.

Urban development deals with the inevitable growth. This growth is subject to the tensions and pressures of three forces: the impact of changes from the outside world, the known developmental factors already at work, and future development policies and alternatives.

The ensuing discussion will touch on the working of these forces. As elaborated later, these factors and policies should shape the growth as well as influence the rate of growth. Specifically, they provide some of the assumptions on which to project future developmental needs and, in turn, the demand on land. The process of conversion is laborious and should belong to the task of a team of master planners. In this paper a quick measure of the scale and broad trend of our city development, by some rough extrapolation of past trends, will be presented in the fifth section. Even then we can only look forward meaningfully to the size and shape of its environment up to the year 1985 and possibly 1990. It is hard to predict up to the year 2000 with comfortable certainty.

The paper will focus on two critical areas of urban development: first, the Central Area, the hub of activities, the keynote to our urban image, the concentration of commercial, financial, administrative, and cultural activities; second, the public housing estates where two-thirds now and eventually over three-quarters of our population will have to make their homes. It attempts to go beyond the question of growth by examining the problems and potentials of the visual and physical design aspects of our city under two further headings: a broad visual survey, looking for key indices of visual changes; and three developmental modes, a persuasion on the importance of considering the interstices in the physical development of the city to enrich our cityscape, out living environment, and our life-style. In this sense, this paper is clearly not a master plan, yet at the same time more than a master plan. It tries to forecast the nature of our urban development in the next two decades, and to identify the potentials of the environment in the next five, ten, and twenty years.

*External Factors*

The smallness of Singapore and the high degree of control of its growth trends have made the island a rather unique urban laboratory. However, this laboratory does not exist in a vacuum. To look forward into the future, we have to assume that the world situation will permit Singapore to maintain its current consistent growth rate, and that our own resources will help us maintain, in one way or another, a constant supply of energy, labour, and construction materials at reasonable cost. Some of the known external forces that planners in Singapore have had to contend with are the energy problem, the economic trend, and tourism.

Our concern over the dwindling oil supply and its rapidly escalating cost has already affected the building design on the one hand and car ownership on the other. New buildings have to observe the OTTV (Overall Thermal Transfer Value) requirements if they are air-conditioned. In time, building materials with low energy input will be given preference. Restraints on car ownership and the engine power of the car will put a continuous pressure on developing a good public transport system. Bus services, however augmented, may still need to be supplemented by the mass transit system. Meanwhile, planners will feel compelled to continue to make the satellite towns as self-contained as possible to minimize travel over long distances.

Economic trends in the world and around the region will affect the speed of our urbanization process, especially in the industrial sector. Active foreign interest in property developments such as housing, shopping, and office premises has led in the past to a quickening of the pace of construction activities and inflation in property values, sometimes coupled with the stimulus for upgrading the quality of buildings. In calculating the rate and directions of growth, our island-state has to reckon with the demands generated by outside investors.

Focusing on a more specific issue, tourism has experienced phenomenal growth in the past decade. Overseas tourists quintupled from 400,000 in 1969 to 2 million in 1978. The number of hotel rooms tripled from 3,700 to 11,500 in the corresponding period. Based on the past trends and barring any worldwide economic depression, we can be guardedly optimistic about the future. Our people and the Government, by then, will probably have to learn to handle the social problems that arise when there are 6 million visitors a year in a country with a population of only 3 million in the year 2000.

It is beyond the scope of this paper to forecast the likely changes in the outside world in the future. For the time being, we take cognition of the importance of this factor and hope that stability will largely prevail to help us continue with our massive experiment in urbanization.

## Internal Factors

In discussing the internal factors, we shall touch on the growth of population and households as related to housing and the impacts of the changing age pyramid and leisure habits.

By virtue of the successful family planning programme, the population is estimated to be expanded by only 27 per cent of the present size to a level of 3 million people by the year 2000. However, despite the reducing population growth rate, that of household remains relatively high, probably by nearly 90 per cent over the same period, reaching an estimated level of 900,000 households. Although it is premature now to project so far ahead, nevertheless if over four-fifths of the total households need public housing, then the Housing and Development Board (HDB) will have to build an additional 400,000 to 450,000 dwelling units in the next twenty years. In other words, what the HDB has built in the last twenty years at about 350,000 dwelling units is less than what is yet to come in the next two decades.

The changing age pyramid affects among others, three areas of the future urban development; namely, the supply of labour force to the industry; the demand on school land; and institutional provisions to the country.

The labour pool will probably increase from 1.5 million to only 2 million from now to the year 2000, whereas it was 0.8 million two decades ago. The slower rate of increase undoubtedly causes concern over its effect on the future rate of industrialization. Qualitative considerations such as new management, new technology, automation, selectivity of new industries can greatly help offset the shorter manpower supply in order to maintain a desirable gross national product (GNP) growth level. This is a good example of how internal and external factors, tempered by policies and alternatives, could influence growth.

In the past ten years, school sites have been provided on the basis that 15 per cent of the population are in primary schools and 10 per cent in secondary schools. According to school enrolment statistics, the percentage of population in primary schools has dropped from 17.4 per cent in 1960 to 12.6 per cent in 1978, and possibly to 10.0 per cent by the year 2000, while that in secondary schools has increased from 3.6 per cent in 1960 to 7.8 per cent in 1978, and perhaps also to 10.0 per cent by the year 2000. This would mean an over-provision in both cases. Again, other qualitative factors come into play. For example, the recent Education Report allows primary schooling to be extended from six to nine years for slower learners. This implies more classes with the same number of pupils. The desire to convert from the double-session school to single-session, to reduce class sizes and to improve pupil-teacher ratio, may justify the present school land reserves.

The demand for the provision of institutions will increase regardless of the age pyramid, but would be influenced by it. For example, in the last few years we saw the establishment of a national art gallery and the refurbishment of our museum. We are in the process of providing a home for our symphony orchestra. And there is even some talk of a cultural centre. On the communal side, the demand for land for religious institutions and associations increases. There has been actually a sudden upsurge of the provision of community centres, kindergartens, polyclinics, welfare centres, and so on. Therefore in Singapore we have to not only provide facilities to match those already existing in the more developed countries but also continuously keep pace with the new demands for facilities in the next twenty years. The changing age pyramid generated the recent proliferation of the homes for the aged and other public health programmes. This seems to be the beginning of the appearance of new social amenities in the years to come.

Although there are no statistics to bear this out, the change in leisure concept means people are beginning to appreciate and make good use of holidays; whereas until recently, a holiday was just a period of time without work. Besides planned vacation, there is an increasing need for recreational grounds near homes for day-to-day use. This will mean more demand for sports facilities and parks in and around the housing estates, new towns, and even places of work. For a change of pace from the highly un-urbanized home environment, there will be greater appreciation of natural parks instead of man-made gardens. In our effort to alleviate the shortage of recreational land, selected offshore islands have already been turned into leisure grounds. If our surrounding seas can be cleaned up soon, a vast outlet for water sports will become available.

## Development Policies and Alternatives

In our urban laboratory, we are fortunate that logical ideas often prevail. The only possible serious constraint on our achievements in urban development is our own limitations in skills and imagination. Our compulsion for logic is most likely to prevail again in the next twenty years. With better experience and expertise accumulated in the last twenty years, our skills will be more varied and refined and our imagination bolder and more relevant. In the near future our city should therefore be more livable and more beautiful.

In looking into the future, we should indeed consciously elevate our visions from one of creating an efficient and well-bleached city to one of creating a city of excellence and richness for gracious living. It should be an ASEAN city in the sense that much of the time, we have to chart our own course and find our own solutions to problems, primarily according to the needs of our own society and region, especially in the context of the Association of Southeast Asian Nations. We have to steer deftly among several conflicting factors. For example, transforming Singapore from an underdeveloped society to a developed country requires enormous social and cultural changes as well as economic upgrading. It requires reconciliation of traditional life style with modern technology. We could aim for a city with our identity. This is not inconceivable. In the last twenty years, we have been innovative in defining our own direction in public housing, in the introduction of car population control and the traffic control through the Area Licensing Scheme in the Central Area. We have demonstrated our ability and therefore should be able to continue to innovate.

In the Central Area, and therefore for the whole island, by far the most exciting thing that we have is the availability of the Marina City for development. There are 600 hectares of reclaimed land under Phases II, V, VI, and VII, as compared with the existing 800 hectares. With this additional land parcel, the various things which our Government could aspire to achieve for our city become easier, though not without difficulties. To mix the old and new is now a more likely

objective, since the pressure to pull down old buildings for more intensive development has eased off. It is a rare chance to plan a twenty-first
century city on the vast new land, to apply our imagination, skills,
and experience to this project.

The idea of working out our own innovations for an ASEAN solution
is more than mere rhetoric. It must surely be the guiding inspiration.
We need bold, non-conforming concepts and creative, clear visions. But
at the same time, we must also understand the nature of practical
problems in order to formulate unerring policies and to find alternatives. On the pragmatic plane, some of the issues that our official
planners will have to face are the land shortage, the relation of urban
development pattern with transportation planning concept, the slum
and squatter clearance, and the pollution alleviation efforts. These
issues will be briefly discussed in this section, which will also include
comments on some aspects of central area, public housing, and industrial developments.

Our awareness of land shortage is far more acute now than ever,
despite the vast expense of greenery still remaining in our island. In
time to come, every piece of land has to be optimized in one way or
another. Even the provision of open space has to be carefully weighed
against other competing uses. In fact this has created a dilemma for
planners in the next twenty years. With increasing pressure for housing
and industrial land, there is also the corresponding increase in recreational land requirements by the sheer increase in population and also
the changing habit of leisure. Critical appraisal of the juxtapositioning
and intensity of land usage is necessary. Constant re-examination of the
land need and staging plan of our island over a long time-frame seems
inevitable. Despite the land shortage, we must have faith that ration-
ality, close planning coordination, and architectural merits can overcome many problems. Above all, we have to try to avoid the common
mistake of hasty development without a clear vision beforehand —
a weakness all too evident in many metropolitan cities.

Although there is no firm government commitment yet, our broad
urban development plans in the last, and hopefully the next, twenty
years were carried out on the assumption that the mass rapid transit
(MRT) system would be undertaken. In fact the island-wide concept
plan is almost tailored exclusively for the system. High density developments along four continuous corridors enhance the viability of the
MRT. However, even if the MRT does not get implemented, this
development model will still greatly help the efficiency, albeit in-
adequately, of a bus service system or other forms of transportation.

Hopefully, while on the subject of transportation, we could examine
possible alternatives for solving traffic congestion problems in the city
centre. The current practice is to continue to widen the roads. This

renders our city more traffic-orientated and less human-orientated. It tends to destroy the fabric of the intimate scale of the older cityscape. We may like to see what parallel efforts are being made in other cities of similar population sizes in order to have an overall, comprehensive review of the Central Area traffic problems by considering the MRT, bus services, existing and future roads, parking policy, the Area Licensing Scheme, etc. Perhaps some of the existing narrow streets in the city can be saved before it is too late. This is only an expression of a wish, in ignorance of the technical problems of transportation planning. Nevertheless, since we are setting targets for the future, we could allow ourselves to indulge in thinking about desirable alternatives. It would be wonderful if we were able to fit a solution to our traffic problem into our vision of an intimate, friendly urban environment.

In all likelihood, the Government will continue to clear slums and squatter areas. The existing dilapidated areas may be expected to be cleared in the next two decades. One may also expect more intensive efforts in pollution control. Although public health services existed a long time ago in Singapore in the form of night soil and refuse collection, drainage, street cleansing, and preventive health measures, there have been fourteen pieces of Legislation and Regulations introduced in the past ten years concerning environmental pollution controls in air, water, and solid wastes. In place of the buckets of nightsoil, at present about 80 per cent of the population enjoy sanitary facilities, compared with 18 per cent in 1960.

The rate of progress depends on two factors, namely, squatter clearance and availability of public sewers. Under the Water Pollution Control and Drainage Act 1975, our Ministry of the Environment can serve notices to occupants or owners of properties without modern sanitation to connect their premises to public sewers. By the end of the century, practically all of the population will be served with modern sanitary facilities.

Given a relatively steady world situation, our Central Area will continue to grow as a commercial, financial, specialized information and tourist centre by virtue of its strategic geographical location and our careful planning of the necessary infrastructures. We believe that the Government will continue with the present policy of keeping the city clean and green. At this point in time, our concept of clean and green means making the city buildings tidy and commodious, decorated and softened with greenery. This policy can be expanded in future by paying greater attention to urban design and street architecture and by the provision of some city squares, small parks, boulevards, and sensibly located landmarks.

In the field of housing, the programme is likely to remain guided by the housing demand of the people as in the past. One of the problems that the Government will probably have to wrestle with is the extent to which we can afford to relax the eligibility rules. A major technical concern is the rapid increase of construction cost which could undermine some of the efforts of improving the residential environment. It is unlikely that our people will ask for more floor space than what a flat by the Housing and Urban Development Company (HUDC) or an HDB executive apartment   provides. However, if inflation does not run wild, residents would in future wish for better building designs and finishing, and less stereotyped landscapes.

Rapid urbanization and population shift in the past decade or two have rendered some of the industrial land provided in the Master Plan outmoded. They are either at the wrong place, with poor accessibility relative to the new population centres and traffic network, or with limited scope for expansion, lacking the complementary activities. As seen from the successive Master Plan revisions, industrial land has not been significantly increased in the past. For this reason, the supply of industrial land will have to be increasingly dependent on the public sector such as the Jurong Town Corporation (JTC) and the HDB. Workers are likely to expect better and more pleasant working conditions, with minimum pollution nuisance. We cannot afford to totally emulate the idea of attractive industrial parks overseas because of the shortage of land. More imaginative site planning and architectural design, however, should help reconcile this dilemma of two contradictory needs, that is, the need to achieve high plot ratio and the need for a more pleasant, greener, and cleaner industrial environment.

## Scale of Future Plans

In this section, we attempt, through the help of published materials to make rough estimates on the scale of new developments required in the next twenty years by extrapolation of the trend of the last twenty years. By this method, with minor adjustments on account of some of the points raised in the previous sections, the probable scale of land used for housing, industry, and commercial developments in the Central Area in the past and future twenty years can be estimated. It is by no means a projection, as this must be left to the competent hands of the government planners.

In the last twenty years, 150 hectares of net commercial land were consumed in the Central Area. It is estimated that another 200 hectares of land in the Central Area will be developed or redeveloped in the next twenty years. For housing, there have been 350,000 private and public housing units built in the last twenty years, consuming 6,500 hectares of gross development land; whereas in the next twenty years there will be again 500,000 dwelling units or 8,000 hectares of land required. To meet the housing demand, the HDB is most likely

# Growth Map - Singapore

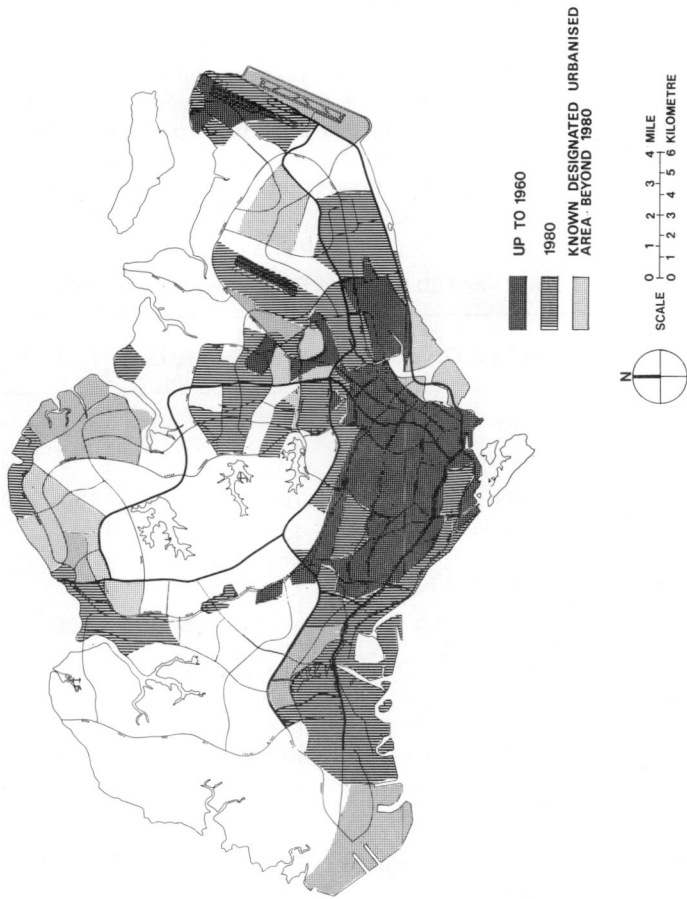

UP TO 1960

1980

KNOWN DESIGNATED URBANISED
AREA BEYOND 1980

SCALE
0  1  2  3  4  MILE
0  1  2  3  4  5  6  KILOMETRE

N

to supply 400,000 to 450,000 units. That means for the next twenty years the HDB has to build the equivalent of ten new towns of the size of 40,000 to 45,000 dwelling units each. In the last twenty years 2,500 hectares of land were developed for industry, whereas in the next twenty years, there could well be another 2,500 hectares or more required.

At present about 20,000 hectares of the Singapore island have been urbanized, with permanent development representing 30 to 35 per cent of the main island. In the next twenty years, it is estimated that about 30,000 to 35,000 hectares or 50 to 55 per cent of the island will be urbanized. Herein lies the reason for careful planning and careful staging of developments. These estimates are summarized in Table 1.

TABLE 1

ESTIMATED NEW DEVELOPMENTS, 1960—2000

| | Estimated New Developments | 1960—1979 | 1980—2000 |
|---|---|---|---|
| 1. | Central Area (Office & Commercial) Net land area* | 150 ha | 150—250 ha |
| 2. | Housing (Private & Public) No. of dwelling units | 350,000 du | 500,000 du |
| | Gross land area | 6,500 ha | 8,000 ha |
| 3. | Industry Gross land area | 2,500 ha | 2,500 ha |
| 4. | Sub Total 1 + 2 + 3 | 9,200 ha | 10,700 ha |
| 5. | Total island-wide urbanized area including pre-1960 development | 18,000 —22,000 ha | 30,000—35,000 ha |
| 6. | % of 5 against total island land area | 30 — 35% | 50 — 55% |

*Excluding land for roads and other uses.

DBS Building — the first of the three 50-storeyed buildings built in the 1970s.

Asia Insurance Building — the tallest office building in early 1960s.

*Great Southern Hotel — built in the mid-1920s.*

*Cathay Building — the tallest hotel in the 1940s and 1950s.*

## A Broad Visual Survey

The old image at the beginning of the 1960s conjures up memories of some of the worst slums and squatter areas this city ever saw. This was so mainly because of the cumulative effects of the sluggish response under the Singapore Improvement Trust (SIT) to housing needs. Even as recent as the early 1970s, in the old Sago Lane area, there were 1,600 persons living in an area of 0.7 hectare, in tiny cubicles in 3- or 4-storeyed low-rise rows of houses which were fire traps. We had our share of the squalid urban squatter colonies, a term hardly used in the last five or six years. One of the last examples was the present Henderson Estate where the density used to be 370 persons per hectare, living in unhygienic shacks. Today, the biggest remaining squatter colony is the Preserverance Estate, with a density of 290 persons per hectare. Clearance action for this Preserverance Estate began in 1973 and is expected to be completed by the early 1980s.

The new visual inputs to our city may be charted by the appearance of certain buildings, complexes, or estates. For example, the Central Area can trace its progress by the proliferation of new office buildings, hotels, and shopping complexes which are not necessarily good or bad, but functional, hygienic, often pleasant, and in general representative of their times. Office buildings have increased not only in height and plot ratio but also in the sophistication of design. For a period of nine years, between 1959 and 1968, Asia Insurance Building reigned supreme as the tallest office building in Singapore. It was overtaken by the 18-storeyed SIA [Singapore Airlines] Building with a more modern look, followed by two 52-storeyed towers known as the OCBC [Oversea-Chinese Banking Corporation] Centre and the DBS [Development Bank of Singapore] Building around 1976.

As for hotels, the Raffles Hotel, the Great Southern Hotel, and the Cathay Hotel were the favourites prior to the Second World War. The Great Southern Hotel was built in the mid-1920s with 38 rooms and 6 storeys. The Cathay Building at 17 storeys claimed to be the tallest hotel in the 1940s and 1950s for about twenty years. Subsequently, the appearance of the Malaysia Hotel (now called the Marco Polo Hotel) in 1965 gave our city some first-class international hotel rooms. After that, there was a mushrooming of more luxurious hotels such as the Mandarin Hotel in 1968 and the Shangri-la Hotel in 1971.

The most popular shopping complex in the 1950s and 1960s was the Robinson Departmental Store in Raffles Place. In the mid-1970s the Plaza Singapura became the first giant one-stop shopping centre.

From now on, not only do we see the further proliferation of such models as the OCBC, Shangri-la, or Plaza Singapura but we also foresee mammoth complexes combining hotels, offices, shops, and entertainment places under one roof, such as the Raffles International Centre and the Marina City projects. Scheduled to be completed around the mid-1980s, each of these projects will yield 250,000 square metres and 500,000 square metres of built-up area respectively. They easily rank among the largest single complexes known in the world at the moment. We have, therefore, demonstrated our financial and technical ability to keep pace with world trends in development in the next two decades, if we choose to. In formulating our image in the future, we do not of course have to follow the trend. It is more important for us to carefully weigh the solutions most desirable for our society and our people.

We cannot speak of the images of Singapore without reference to public housing estates; after all, over two-thirds of the developed lands in the past and the next two decades are put to this use. Broadly speaking, in physical planning and design, the HDB has gone through four or five stages of developments. In the early years of the 1960s, it went through a period of emergency building, characterized by vigorous efforts to assemble land, especially in the urban fringe, and to build as many units as possible in the shortest possible time, at as high a density as our construction or lift technology would permit. By so doing, the momentum of our public housing and urban redevelopment could then be picked up and sustained. This was thus the catalyst-making formative period.

For the rest of the decade, a series of prototype flats, definitely our own, was evolved, with unmistakable features like the bathrooms and toilets leading off the kitchens, among others. This could be called a period of consolidation of early experiments.

Then, in the 1970s, it again went through a period of refinement. Floor plans, building specifications and, more importantly, planning standards and criteria were improved. Responding to the need for speedy construction, and constrained by the shortage of manpower and relative inexperience of our workers, the HDB had to resort to a high degree of standardization. The design emphasis then was to design consistently well-functioning flats set in a neat and pleasant environment. This was a period of design discipline, as a preparation for a more exciting era in the 1980s. With guidelines and criteria already well tested, and with the increased experience of the HDB's professional staff and private contractors, the next decade should be a period of more confident experimentations and explorations, not only in variations in building design but also in the combination of various building heights and the search for complementary physical solutions as responses to social needs.

The significant projects in the last two decades include the Bukit Ho Swee, executed in the formative period, the Toa Payoh New Town, often referred to as a prototype for new towns in Singapore, a product of the foundation-laying period. This prototype was further refined in

*Raffles International Centre — a mammoth complex of hotels, offices, shops, and entertainment places under one roof with 250,000 sq. metres of floor area.*

*Bukit Ho Swee Estate — one of the first public housing estates built by HDB in early 1960s during the formative period.*

*Toa Payoh — a prototype HDB New Town in late 1960s and early 1970s.*

the Ang Mo Kio New Town, a model for the future new towns in Singapore. In Ang Mo Kio, one can see the fusion of design standard and criteria on the one hand, and design discipline on the other. Neatness, pleasantness, and functionality are the hallmarks which belonged to the 1970s. For the next decade or so, it is hoped that the new efforts and new visions can be adequately expressed through the proposed Tampines New Town. A new planning tool will be introduced into the plans of new towns for at least the next six to eight years. Known as the precincts, they are subdivisions of a neighbourhood, each with its own communal focal points. There are many more ideas being explored and tested, in preparation for the eighties and possibly the nineties. These ideas, if successful, should make our residential environment more livable, and the visual images more varied.

As for the town centres, the first example was Queenstown Town Centre built in 1969. However, the prototype using pedestrian malls as linkages, and putting car parks and loading and unloading facilities out of sight of shoppers, can be traced to Toa Payoh Centre and the Marine Parade Phase I Neighbourhood Centre. These two centres also bear the characteristics of the 1970s, that is, discipline and neatness. However, by 1979, we see the emergence of Bedok Town Centre, modelled on Toa Payoh Town Centre but more enriched in spatial and visual qualities. It signals the new orientation of our designers in the 1980s.

The first attempt in the Central Area by the HDB was the Selegie House where the density was an impressive 2,500 persons per hectare. This density was never repeated later. However, the project serves the purpose of resettling people affected by public projects. This was followed by the first prototype of public housing sitting on a podium, the Outram Park built in 1970. A refined version of it is the Waterloo Centre, where the podium is better integrated with high-rise structures, and an attempt is made to break the box-like appearance of the podium. We are looking forward to the completion of Kreta Ayer Complex by 1983, where personality and characteristics can be much more readily discerned. The design is to move from the purely functional shape to one of architectural expression in order to enhance the quality of the cityscape. Another example is the Albert Centre where the design is not only more exciting but also a first attempt at introducing a regional flavour by exploring Chinese architectural characteristics. It is hoped that there will be further attempts in this direction, and that the new buildings will be less imitative and more interpretive of the regional architectural styles.

The transformation of industrial estates can be summed up by comparing the examples of Geylang Square and Geylang East. In the Geylang Square, the terrace workshops can be seen from Sims Avenue, one of the main roads. The flatted factories were designed purely as a functional entity. On the other hand, in Geylang East, the design of the terrace workshops was refined. And even then, they are effectively screened off from view by the much more attractive four-storeyed industrial shops. The architectural efforts made by many local and overseas industrialists on land parcels leased from the Government have generally further enhanced the landscape of the industrial areas. With the emphasis on higher technology, the quality of industrial buildings and their surroundings can only continue to improve.

### Three Developmental Modes

The previous section gave a broad review and preview of our urban image. However, the quality of a city does not depend just on these landmark projects or mass-produced environments. If, in the more developed countries, the demand of their people for environmental improvements is any guide at all, Singaporeans will ask for enrichment of the environment in the next decades too. The character of a city is achieved over a period of centuries. It may not be readily apparent in a modern city such as Singapore despite its history of a hundred and fifty years.

To give our cityscape more character, there should be more than just a parade of large-parcelled complexes but also quaint old buildings, historical spots, intriguing side lanes, and variations in visual forms and spaces. Let us take a hypothetical situation. If a city consists of nothing else but large-parcelled complexes, these solid structures would stay for scores of years. Then, theoretically, there would be no room for growth. The city as well as the cityscape would practically be a museum. It would not be an exciting museum since the exhibits reflect similar aesthetic tastes and technology. It is bad enough to turn a city into a museum; it is worse if the collection is limited in artistic expressions. After all, it is not necessarily true that what's large or new must be better. In a city, we need variety in our environment, mixing the large and the small, the old and the new. Otherwise, the city would become predictable and impersonal, and therefore dull and shallow.

At the same time, it takes many more human minds, professionals and non-professionals, through repeated refinement and creativity, care and love, to give sustaining interest and beauty to a city, a place where one could explore again and again and discover new things. Whereas we may find comfort and efficiency in the new and large complexes, we still have to seek this more durable quality of a city. A city of excellence involves more than mere expansion, more than efficiency and pleasantry. It must be growing all the time, like a living organism. It involves more than all the skills of clever professionals and requires the efforts of the owners and users of the buildings.

*Ang Mo Kio — a neat, pleasant, and functional New Town reflecting the faithful application of our complete set of planning criteria and design guidelines prepared by the HDB during the early 1970s.*

*Albert Centre — a new image of public housing in the Central Area.*

*Geylang East — industrial shops can be good looking.*

*People's Park and People's Park Complex — mixed development based on the pedestrian mall concept.*

It would seem then that if these objectives are to be achieved, the mode of development must be a simultaneous three-pronged effort. The first, obviously, is the large parcelled developments such as the URA [Urban Renewal Authority] sales of sites or the HDB housing estates for slum and squatter clearance, and to meet new social and economic needs. The importance and indispensability of these techniques can surely be seen in the vastly upgraded living conditions in the city. The second, being development in a special sense, is the preservation of the heritage which we cherish, be it old buildings or entire districts, but not necessarily monuments. For whatever we pull down cannot be replaced. No amount of skilful modern architecture can compensate for the monotony of a city which has been built within a short span of time. There are about 1.2 million square metres of such old buildings in the Republic — approximately a third of the total annual yield of new floor area by the HDB. The problem is small and the expenditure incurred should be within our means. New legislation is required. So far the few attempts at rehabilitating old buildings come mainly from the Government. If the Government spells out a clear policy, private sector participation may be expected, thereby reducing the burden of the Government.

These two elements, the large complexes and historical spots, to a city are like exhibits in an urban museum. For they are not to be substantially altered or modified in the short run. Apart from human activities, to maintain the city as a living organism, we have to leave enough existing structures interspersed; these may not be good and may thus be altered, modified, or demolished and developed or redeveloped at any time.

Out of the three modes, the first two are familiar techniques, much discussed. The third has been adopted in Singapore. However, the importance of this seemingly unglamorous mode of development must be duly recognized. Small projects such as the Handicraft Centre, Changi Village, and several charming small hotels add spice to our cityscape and city life. Buildings such as those along Robinson Road and the commercial buildings, including the old Majestic Theatre, which grew around a common pedestrian mall at the People's Park Complex, enrich our city.

For the Central Area as a whole, obviously the Marina City will be the new city, reflecting essentially the latest concept in large-parcelled complexes. It would be ideal, though requiring much patience and skill, if certain parts could be allowed to grow at a slightly different pace. By the same token, the existing downtown is the "old" city, possessing the potential of all the charms of an environment developed with the three modes. Our planners can fully exploit the different advantages of these two new and old areas and create a Singapore which is complex, varied,

Model of a Precinct Layout being implemented in Tampines New Town, where it is easier for the residents to perceive their physical and social identity.

embracing the latest as well as the old, the modest and the small projects. For a large-parcelled development project, one could, by carefully delineating the boundaries of development, strive to allow old buildings to exist side by side with new complexes.

It is not easy to achieve these goals in a modern city like Singapore. Time is required to gradually bring about the enrichment. But our vision, creativity, and skills should be allowed to expand. We have to be committed to this course. For if we falter, we shall not be able to create a great city. It may be added that in pursuing this three-pronged development, the individual urban design and architectural merits certainly play a decisive role in the quality of our visual environment.

Departing from the Central Area and considering the housing field, let us discuss the application of this concept to some of the HDB projects implemented recently or to be implemented in the near future. In the Guillemard Estate Redevelopment Project, most of the existing two-storey residential blocks seem to be in good condition. The general surroundings are pleasant. Therefore, high-rise blocks have been built only in the land parcels where dilapidated structures have been demolished. The end result is a mixed landscape, more interesting than an estate of new buildings. This is an example of growth in the interstitial spaces in residential estates. This approach is carried through and expanded in some Central Area projects where certain interesting and sound old buildings are maintained, interspersed with the proposed high-rise buildings. Thus the plan incorporates the possibility of the three-pronged development.

An HDB housing estate or new town can be said to be deprived in the sense that, in virtually all cases, there can only be the two-pronged approach — the large-parcelled development and the growth in interstitial spaces. There is little or nothing that is part of our heritage. Even the question of growth is limited to the simple means of reserving parcels of land in the neighbourhood for future development or for public tenders for commercial, industrial, or institutional development. Because of the urgency of the public housing programme and the difficulties in land acquisition and clearance, generally, there have been very few reserved sites available for growth. The industrial areas and the town centres take up most of the reserved land parcels. And there are also a few at strategic corners of an estate or new town. There are not enough sites to provide sufficiently for the future enrichment of the residential environment. The character of each estate, however, will vaguely and timidly emerge over the next decades. It is of course the hope of the HDB planners to reserve more sites in the future.

However, there are other ways to create interest and variety in the housing environment too. For example, the need for more relaxed gathering spots for the residents of HDB estates is partly met by the development of the neighbourhood centres, the shopping and communal focal points with plazas and malls for people to gather, or the town gardens such as that in Toa Payoh.

Throughout the new town, the surroundings can be improved through the use of the precinct concept. Precinct, in the HDB context, is a subdivision of a neighbourhood. The smaller areas are more manageable and allow the residents to perceive and maintain their identity. An activity focal point in the centre of the precinct is provided, in the form of a landscaped square wherein recreational facilities, gardens, eating houses, and local retail shops can be located. Hopefully, the architects can provide for each precinct to evolve its own identity. A new town should be enriched if it is planned according to this concept — more varied and interesting, with a stronger sense of growth. Ideally, if land is available, HDB planners should deliberately leave out certain precincts to be developed years later, to achieve growth in the original sense of the word. The precinct idea, coupled with reserved sites, should make the new towns of tomorrow more beautiful, not to mention the better urban design and architecture which have been promised.

For both the Central Area and the public housing estates, the images for the next two decades are substantially better than they were twenty years ago. We can optimistically look forward to more creativity. As long as we continue to think rationally in the urban laboratory, as long as we want our skills and creativities to grow and develop, and as long as we aim for excellence, we should be able to attain our environmental goals.

# 7

# Impact of Technological Changes and Developments

### R.S. Bhathal

If a visionary in the 1930s had predicted that Singapore's spectacular economic growth in the 1970s would be based on the physics and technology of the first industrial revolution, he may have been proven right. However, he would have been proven wrong if he had tried to predict the speed with which technology would enter Singapore.

In such circumstances, one can only forecast some trends based on certain assumptions which one hopes will not change too drastically. We shall not be concerned very much about predicting new technological products. The reason for this is that the rapid increase in new technological products makes prediction both difficult and uncertain. The early futurologists who were working in the 1960s took a simplistic approach — that of extrapolating current trends. However, most of their predictions of future technological achievements today appear completely out of date. This is not because the few years since they were drawn up have made it clear that some of the innovations then envisaged are unlikely to be possible but because of a change of attitude towards technology. Instead of asking only what we shall do, we now ask how we shall do it, for whom, with what resources and what consequences.

In this paper we shall, therefore, look at the rate at which technology is entering Singapore, the rate of technological development in the science and technology system, and the impact of these changes as Singapore moves towards the year 2000.

*Rate of Technology Entry*

In 1879 the electric lamp was invented. Twenty-seven years later, the first 48 lights turned night into day in the city of Singapore. This single invention was to have a tremendous impact on both the social and economic life of people here. As Singapore's urbanization programme got underway in the 1960s the electric lamps were to serve as beacons of light as the hundreds of high-rise buildings spotted the night landscape. They have become the symbols of the modern city, as the cathedrals and temples were the emblems of pre-industrial life. Today, we take tourists to see Toa Payoh — the achievement of the processes of science and technology.

Another unknown man, in 1903, flew the world's first powered, manned, heavier-than-air craft. The plane flew for 12 seconds and for about 30 metres. Sixteen years later, in 1919 the first aeroplane the Vickers Vimy landed at Farrer Park on its way from England to Australia. In 1969, the Concorde which flies at supersonic speeds made its appearance in the field of aviation. About 8 years later on 10 December 1977 the Concorde landed in Singapore from England.

In 1945, Presper Eckert and John Mauchly of the University of Pennsylvania unveiled ENIAC (Electronic Numerical Integrator and Computer), the first digital computer to be designed entirely along electronic principles. The computer was enormous. It weighed more than 30 tons, contained 18,800 vacuum tubes with half a million connections (these connections took Eckert and Mauchly two and a half years to solder), a vast network of resistors, and miles of wiring. It could perform about 5,000 computations a second. It started the computer revolution. Twenty-three year later, the first computer was installed in Singapore.

Then in 1970 the microprocessor was born in the United States. The microprocessor chip 4004 or the microcomputer MCS-4 just about matched ENIAC's computational power and the capability of an IBM machine of the early 1960s. About 8 years later, the microprocessor was found in the market place here. Today, tertiary college students are beginning to play with the microprocessor and trying to appreciate its applications and capabilities. It will be noticed that the speed at which "new" technology has been entering into Singapore has been decreasing (i.e., from 27 years to 8 years). It is unlikely that this will cease in the years ahead since Singapore has an open economy and allows the flow of technology and technical manpower across its national boundary.

*The Technological System*

To understand the rate of technological growth one has to appreciate the scientific and technological system. It is unlikely that the rate at which technological products make their way to the market place is going to slow down. This is partly due to the fact that while the percentage growth of the economy in advanced countries is increasing at the rate of about 3 per cent, certain industries with large investments in research and development (R & D) are growing at about 15 to 25 per cent. The technological system had obsolescence built into it. For most of human history the norm has been continuity. But with technology, this is not so. The German mathematician David Hilbert was quite correct when he observed that the importance of scientific work can be measured by the number of previous publications it makes super-fluous to read. Scientists and technologists dare not wait for their current journals. They must study "preprints" and become members of the "Invisible College" just to make sure that their work has not become obsolete by what somebody else has done overnight.

The science and technology system is a world of obsolescence. Buildings are torn down to make way for parking lots, offices, houses, etc. Progress seems to have become quick, sudden, and almost whole-sale.

Our attitudes to change have changed. Today, nations are distin-guished not by their monuments but by their pace of change. We don't talk of "civilized" or "uncivilized" nations. Today, we use the words "developing" and "developed" nations, and use a common standard to measure the convergence of nations to a common standard of living. That is, we use gross national product (GNP), per capita annual income, and rates of growth to measure the success of a country. In fact, when one visits a foreign country today one wants to know whether the water is drinkable, whether the electrical voltage is constant, whether there is a telephone service which works, whether there is colour television, whether cars are available, whether there is modern sanita-tion, etc. One begins to grade the country against a technological index.

The technological system is an irreversible system. It cannot be un-invented. No one wants (unless he is an incurable romantic) to go back to the days of the kerosene lamp or the smoky wood fire. The electric lamp has been invented and we use it with great delight. While any technological device can be made obsolete it cannot, however, be forgotten. Motorcars (although we are aware of the problems they cause) cannot be removed with one fell swoop. All we do is build parking temples on choice urban real estate and let the car pass under pedestrian overpasses. Another invention which we can't do away with seems to be television. The technology of television seems to bring us together and, at the same time, to find a new way of separating us from one another. The world of Singaporeans in the year 2000 will be a world of private compartments. The natural progressions of technol-ogy are already here and will intensify in future, that is, the progres-sion from the intimately jostling rickshaw to the tram-car to the lone driver of a car; the progression of the parent reading aloud to the children to the darkened cinema to the home television set, etc.

### Shift in Technology

Once a country has decided to industrialize, it is set on acquiring technology to make more technology possible. That is, it has also begun to assimilate into the science and technology system.

Until the late 1950s, Singapore depended primarily on its entrepot trade and commercial activities. Their dependence on trade made the people outward-looking and receptive to new ideas and changes in the environment. This attitude of mind prepared the ground for the assimilation of new technology that began to flow into the country when Singapore decided to industrialize in 1959. In the early sixties the manufacturing sector accounted for about 9 per cent of the gross domestic product (GDP), and it employed about 27,000 workers. The technological products were based mainly on textiles, food, beverages, footwear, and leather industries.

From the mid-sixties to the early seventies Singapore began to attract multinational companies to set up base here. It was a time when multinational companies were looking for low-cost areas to assemble their products. The desires of both partners coincided and Singapore prospered with the "new" technology industries. The "new" technology industries represented the "modern" industries of the last fifty years in the advanced countries.

By the late seventies there was a gradual shift from the labour-intensive to the more skill-intensive industries. There was a shift to petroleum, chemicals, plastics, electronics, electrical and precision optical products. Manufacturing accounted for over 21 per cent of the GDP and employed about 220,000 workers.

With the prospect that Singapore will not be able to compete in the long run with lower-cost countries in labour-intensive industries, Singapore in mid-1979 has adopted a strategy to promote high-technology industries and services. This is similar to the strategy followed by Western advanced nations in the thirties when they found that they could no longer compete with Japan in labour-intensive industries (textiles, footwear, toys, etc.), in which wages for unskilled work are the major cost. In a developed economy, unskilled labour is a gross misallocation of the most productive and most expensive of all economic resources, the human resource. The Japanese later found that they could no longer remain competitive in these industries, compared to Hong Kong, Taiwan, Korea, etc. So the industries moved out to these countries. To curb the expansion of unskilled jobs and to provide a tighter control over the import of unskilled workers, a high-wage policy has been adopted in Singapore.

*Towards the Year 2000*

Having noted the rate of technology entry into Singapore, some aspects of the technology system, and the shift in technology in Singapore's industrial system, let us now see what the future trends will be as Singapore moves towards the year 2000.

In order to do this we need to make certain assumptions. It is not likely that Singaporeans will lose their desire to enjoy the products of science and technology. Most of them will remain sufficiently motivated to work for these in order to enjoy greater affluence. They will also be willing to upgrade their skills to provide mobility up the technological ladder.

It is also assumed that there will be no barriers to the flow of technology into the country from the advanced countries. It is assumed that the advanced countries will always find that some of their technological products could be more cheaply produced in the developing countries or the newly industrializing countries.

It is further assumed that the advanced countries will continue to produce new technology and the recent concern that the spirit of invention is declining is more imagined than real. It is also assumed that we shall continue to have a constant supply of energy.

During the next decade, Singapore's development strategy to attract high-technology industries will be successful as the groundwork is now being laid. The manufacturing output will in the future be concentrated in the petroleum, petrochemical, electronics, aerospace (repair and servicing), and precision industries. A majority of these firms will be owned by companies from the advanced nations as these will help in the transfer of the technology.

In keeping with the desire to assimilate advanced technology, Singapore has started to set up a "science park". It is hoped that the park, to be located near the university will attract high-technology industries to set up R & D laboratories. In the next twenty years, the productivity of scientists and engineers will change as the university and other research departments are revamped. The process of reorganization of the research system has begun and will gather momentum in the years ahead.

In the 1960s Singapore will move into the more advanced stages of high technology industries such as aerospace (manufacturing), computing, and telecommunications. These will be supported by the knowledge-based, information-handling professions and occupations. The primary industries have virtually disappeared from the Singapore scene while the secondary and tertiary industries have come to play a more important role in Singapore's economic growth. The manufacturing sector will probably increase to occupy about 30 per cent of the GDP while the service industries will begin to play a more important role as Singapore nears the year 2000. Personal and social services, including the provision of care, amenity, and entertainment will continue to become more institutionalized and professionalized.

Because Singapore is plugged into the science and technology system, the existing trends of assimilating technology will continue to accelerate. By relying on advanced technology and automation, Singaporeans will be able to further their limits of acquiring material wealth. Although much has been written and talked about the computer, it has not really changed the average person's life-style to the extent cars and home electricity did in the forty years following their respective introduction. While computer companies are selling computers they are not selling them at the rate of the electric lamp. What is lacking is not a piece of hardware such as the electric lamp. What has still to be created is the conceptual understanding of information. As long as every set of data has to be laboriously translated into a separate "programme" we will not be able to understand information.

However, this situation will have improved in the next twenty years. The impact of cheap, reliable, fast, and universally available information will be as great as was the impact of electricity on the lives of the man in the street. Young people will by then be using information systems as their normal tools, much as they now use the typewriter or the telephone. Yet the telephone about sixty years ago evoked somewhat the same panic the computer now does. By the 1990s, it is safe to predict, people will have learnt that the computer is a powerful tool, and that it enables them to do the mind work they want to do and are unable to do today for want of cheap, reliable, and fast information. The information industry will create a new set of employment opportunities.

In the 1960s, computer scientists expected artificial intelligence research and related activities to yield insights into human intelligence. However, many goals the scientists thought would be met by the 1970s may not be met well into the 1980s. Robots have been on the industrial scene since the 1960s but the first models were big affairs designed mainly for difficult and harzadous jobs. The newer ones that are appearing in industrial laboratories and some factories in the advanced countries are smaller and brainier. They have been helped by the introduction of the microprocessor whose capabilities have yet to be utilized fully. Industrial robotics is a technology which will begin to be introduced on the Singapore industrial scene in the late 1990s. They will replace some of the blue-collar work force in the more repetitive tasks which are presently being done by them. This will not cause any serious dislocation as these people will be retrained for other jobs.

Since obsolescence and specialization are characteristics of the technology system, the work force will need to be retrained. What is learnt in schools, colleges, and universities will have to be updated as soon as the worker begins to work in a factory or an office. Ever since Adam Smith, economists have told us that it is highly efficient to specialize because, as Paul Samuelson's classic textbook puts it, it is "better for fat men to do the fishing, lean men the hunting, and smart men to make the medicine. . . ." Industrial societies have carried the division of labour to extreme degrees. The growth of the industrial society in Singapore has given rise to a social structure characterized by the division of labour and social mobility. There are now over 1,000 titles and job descriptions in Singapore where there were less than 100 in the agricultural and trading community 150 years ago. Advancing technology in Singapore will require more division of labour and specialization. The demand for varied new products and services will bring with it a proliferation of varied new work processes, and alternative work routines for both blue- and white-collar workers.

The growth of the industrial society in Singapore will also pull more women out of their homes. This will mainly be to increase the household income to enjoy the consumer products· of the industrial society and the leisure that it gives. With two incomes young couples will travel outside Singapore more than they do today. This will in turn give rise to other leisure industries to satisfy the needs of the new Singaporean.

## Conclusion

The last twenty years have seen the influx of technology and the acquisition of new skills by both blue- and white-collar workers. The next twenty years will see a further influx of technology but at a higher level. It will also see an influx of more scientific and technical manpower so that Singapore by the year 2000 will have the greatest concentration of technical manpower in this region. It will also have graduated by then into the league of the advanced nations, and its people will enjoy a per capita income of about S$30,000, which will be similar to that of some of the advanced countries.

Just as Venice served as a dynamic centre for Europe during the Renaissance period, so will Singapore serve as the city of the future in Southeast Asia, that is, Singapore will be the technological city, the commercial city, and perhaps the cultural city of Southeast Asia in the year 2000.

# 8

## Energy Options and Their Implications

Singapore has no indigenous energy resources whatsoever. On the other hand, Singapore, like all other great cities of this technological and industrial age, depends heavily on an adequate supply of energy for its survival and continuing progress. Without energy all that tremendous development that had taken place over the last twenty years or so would not have been possible. Without energy this great metropolis would grind to a standstill.

To meet its present energy requirements, Singapore depends entirely on imported petroleum products. All the power stations use fossil fuel oil. Town gas is produced from Naphtha — a by-product of the refining process of crude oil. Diesel and petrol are used for transportation as well as for industrial plants. Liquefied petroleum gas (LPG) is used as a supplement to town gas principally for cooking purposes. Currently, Singapore consumes approximately 3.2 million tonnes of imported petroleum products per year, worth close to a billion dollars in foreign exchange. It has a per capita consumption of 1.35 tonnes which is the second highest in Asia after Japan. The increase in energy consumption is estimated at around 6 per cent a year, so that in ten years' time the consumption figure is likely to reach 5.7 million tonnes.

This total dependence on imported petroleum products does not place us in a very comfortable position. It means that we are very susceptible to the effects of fuel oil politics and fuel oil price escalation. The 1973 fuel oil crisis and the more recent Iranian problem amply demonstrated how vulnerable we are to events which are completely beyond our control. Even without any crises, liquid fossil fuel is a rapidly diminishing commodity, and it has been predicted that by the turn of the century fuel oil will become so scarce, if available at all, and the price will be so high that it will not be conceivable to burn it as fuel. In the longer term, therefore, it is not a sound strategy to continue our total dependence on petroleum products to meet our energy requirements.

Some people seem to derive comfort from the fact that we are the third largest fuel oil refining centre in the world, and erroneously assume that the mere presence of the number of refineries will assure us of an uninterrupted supply of fuel oil. Nothing can be further from the truth. The refineries do not produce fuel oil, they merely process it. Their presence will not protect us from the spectre of fuel oil shortage and astronomical escalations in fuel oil price. What we need to do is to use the time between now and when fuel oil becomes really scarce and expensive to wean ourselves away from fuel oil and to evolve alternative energy options to ensure our continuing progress and survival.

Having stated the need for energy alternatives, let us consider what options are available and what the implications are. Based on present-day technology and taking into consideration the peculiarity of our own circumstances, the options that are available may be listed as follows: nuclear, coal, natural gas, solar, wind and ocean, others including refuse, bio-gas, and alcohol, and lastly, power import. Let us consider each option in greater detail and examine its implications.

## Nuclear

Nuclear energy has been variously hailed as the ultimate solution to the world's energy problems or as the doomsday instrument which will finally destroy the world. Neither extreme is true. Nuclear power is an established technology and many nuclear power reactors have indeed been in operation for years, supplying electrical energy successfully in many countries. Advocates of nuclear power will tell you that nuclear power is clean, it is statistically safe, and a pound of uranium has more energy than a train load of coal. With such overwhelming and apparent advantages, why have we not adopted nuclear energy to solve our problem?

Indeed we examined the possibility of using nuclear energy as early as the early 1970s, well before the fuel oil crisis of 1973. The findings of our investigation were that while nuclear power certainly had its advantages, its application was not without problems and difficulties, and on balance it was not as attractive as it first appeared. The special difficulties and problems, especially in the context of our own situation, are the vast investment required, the size of the system, the complexity of nuclear fuel supply, and the lack of a suitable site.

### Vast Investment Required

For a variety of complex reasons, nuclear power hardwares are unbelievably expensive. When we talk about investment in nuclear power we are talking about committing the nation to an investment of a magnitude which can seriously affect its financial standing, particularly when the nation is a small one like ours. The 660 MW nuclear power plant under construction in the Philippines, for instance, costs the equivalent of S$2.6 billion nominally, and this order was placed some three years ago.

To build such a nuclear plant, each of us will, on the average, have to invest more than S$1,000. The output of this unit will meet only roughly half our present electrical energy requirement. With the same amount of money, we can build about 3,000 MW of oil burning plants or 2,300 MW of coal burning plants, more than adequate for our electrical energy requirement to 1990.

Incidentally, from the standpoint of security and reliability of supply, it is not a good arrangement to build only one nuclear power unit. It should rightly be backed up by a second unit. If this is done we are talking about roughly doubling the investment to S$5 billion. The implications in risking such a vast investment are obvious.

The size of the investment in capital equipment is not the only obstacle. Going nuclear means going into an entirely new area of technology in which we have little or no expertise. This means we will have to invest in manpower and training, which can be a very expensive business. Furthermore, with our small population base, can we really afford to tie up a substantial number of our high calibre engineers, technologists, and scientists solely to cater to the numerous facets of operating a nuclear power plant?

## Size of System

For a nuclear power plant to be economically competitive with conventional fossil fuel plants, it has to be of a minimum size so that economies of scale may be obtained. Currently, the minimum size is about 600 MW, or the standard commercial size of 660 MW, such as the one being built in the Philippines.

This constraint on minimum size poses a serious problem for comparatively small electrical systems such as ours. We have at present a maximum system load of around 1,100 MW. If we have a nuclear power unit in operation, the output of this unit would account for approximately 50 per cent of the total system load. Should anything malfunction and this unit automatically disconnects itself from the supply system instantaneously, half the nation will be without a supply of electricity. In fact the situation could be far more serious. Because such a large chunk of load is instantaneously disconnected, the stability of the electrical network would be seriously affected. The resulting surge would probably cause all the other generating units to automatically disconnect themselves from the supply system. This means total power supply failure to the whole nation. Such a situation is obviously unacceptable. In fact for security and reliability of supply, it is prudent never to allow the size of the largest unit in the system to exceed about 25 per cent of the total system load. In other words, even if nuclear power were in every other way desirable, because of the minimum size constraint we cannot consider the installation of a unit until our system load has reach 2,500 MW or thereabout.

## Complexity of Nuclear Fuel Supply

The present generation of nuclear power reactors use uranium as fuel. Uranium as a resource is not abundantly available and is equally prone to depletion as liquid fossil fuel oil. Like fuel oil, the price of uranium has also undergone sharp escalations in recent years, although it is acknowledged that because of the very much smaller quantities involved the operating cost of a nuclear power reactor is less sensitive to escalation in price of its fuel than a conventional fossil fuel plant.

Liquid fuel oil can be used for power production after undergoing a relatively simple process of refining in facilities widely available all over the world. Uranium however cannot. The uranium ore must undergo complicated refining processes and be fabricated into nuclear fuel rods before it can be used in a nuclear power reactor. At present the technology and facilities available for the refining of uranium and fabrication of fuel rods are limited to a small number of advanced industrialized countries. The position is even worse in the case of light water reactors where enrichment of the fuel is required. Because of the high level of technology and the vast amount of capital involved, only very few countries have fuel enrichment facilities. The supply of nuclear power reactor fuel is thus prone to political and other non-commercial complications.

Switching from liquid fossil fuel oil to nuclear power is actually switching from one precarious resource to another equally precarious one, and transferring one's dependence on the oil producing countries to the even more limited number of highly industrialized countries.

## Lack of a Suitable Site

Perhaps the most difficult problem relating to the application of nuclear power in the context of our own situation is the lack of a suitable site for a nuclear power station. Statistically, nuclear power reactors are remarkably safe. They have had indeed an impressive safety record. Nevertheless, notwithstanding all the built-in safeguards, there is always the million-to-one chance that something can go wrong. By this we do not mean a nuclear explosion. A nuclear power station cannot explode like an atomic bomb. The worst possible case would be the melt-down of the reactor core with attendant release of massive doses of radioactivity. This is popularly referred to as the "China Syndrome". However, because of the extreme toxicity of radioactive gases, one need not have a "China Syndrome" to have problems. Even what would normally be considered as minor leaks could pose serious safety and health hazards, given the combination of circumstances. For this reason, nuclear power stations are located as far as possible from population centres and are usually isolated by an exclusion zone followed by another low population density zone. The rationales are, firstly, to risk as few people to radiation exposure as possible and, secondly, in the event of a leak, to be able to evacuate people to a safe area.

Because we have such a heavy population concentration, there is not available a site sufficiently remote to accommodate a nuclear power station. The recent Three Mile Island incident clearly demonstrated the kind of problem one can encounter with the operation of nuclear power plant. Had the incident occurred in a small country, with a heavy concentration of population with no means of evacuation, the anxiety and fear that would have been caused could well be imagined.

Because of the foregoing reasons, it has been decided not to go into nuclear power for the time being. This decision has proven to be correct in the light of recent developments. However, we should not rule out nuclear power forever. Other possibilities exist and the technology is developing all the time. One that has often been mentioned is that of fusion — nuclear energy without the attendant risk of radioactivity. A lot of research is being done in this area, but no break-through seems to be in sight. The prospect of fusion nuclear energy playing a significant role even by the turn of the century seems remote at the present moment.

### Coal

Coal has been used as fuel through the centuries. It was the fuel that sustained the great industrial revolution and could have continued to play the dominant role had it not been for the emergence of fuel oil. Because of the ready availability and convenience of fuel oil use, coal was edged out of the fuel market in the last thirty years or so. With few exceptions, the coal industry was left very much in the doldrums.

Nevertheless, coal as an industrial fuel has the advantage of a well-established technology, and there exists a wealth of accumulated expertise in this field. It is not surprising, therefore, that since the fuel oil crisis of 1973, there has been a resurgence of interest in the use of coal as an industrial fuel. Many new power plants are planned or being built to burn coal instead of fuel oil.

There is a definite swing towards the increasing use of coal in the future years. Apart from the fact that the use of coal relies on a well-proven technology, there are other factors which favour the selection of coal as our alternative fuel. These are the relative abundance in supply, the wider spread in distribution, and the lower cost.

## Relative Abundance in Supply

As a world resource, coal is definitely more abundant in supply than fuel oil. Whereas it has been estimated that fuel oil will be depleted by the turn of the century, there is enough coal to meet requirements for the next two hundred years or so. The accuracy of the two estimates have often been questioned, but in fact is not particularly important. The difference between the two is of such an order of magnitude that it should be patently clear that, generally speaking, switching over to coal means placing reliance on a more reliable source of fuel supply.

## Wider Spread in Distribution

Whereas fuel oil is found in few areas of the world, with most being concentrated in the middle east countries, coal resources are found to be more evenly and widely distributed all over the world. The implications are that, firstly, one has a wider choice of sources from which to purchase coal and, secondly, there is a smaller likelihood of so many widely-dispersed countries with supplies of coal forming a cartel to manipulate coal prices.

These factors, coupled with the relative abundance already mentioned, should result in a more stable supply in terms of availability and cost.

## Lower Cost

Cost of energy per unit derived from coal is lower than the same derived from fuel oil. It is true that when fuel oil price goes up the price of coal is likely to go up as well. However, because of the relative abundance factor it is not expected that coal price will escalate as fast as that of fuel oil. Conversely, towards the end of the century, it is expected that fuel oil will be priced so high that no one can afford to burn it as a fuel but it will be reserved for use as a feedstock for petrochemical process.

The use of coal, however, is not without problems. Based on present conditions the problems are the lack of a large-scale international trade, inflexibility in the use of coal, and pollution caused by its use.

## Lack of a Large-scale International Trade

For the present there is no international trade in coal of a scale anywhere near that of fuel oil. For fuel oil, one can very conveniently invite bids for its supply from a large number of international oil companies. The same cannot as yet be applied to the purchase of coal.

Coal contracts are usually concluded on a bilateral basis between the purchaser and the mine owner. International coal transportation is yet another problem. The number of bulk coal carriers are few compared to the abundant oil tankers and supertankers. It is expected, however, that these are transitory weaknesses. Once the coal trade picks up on a substantial scale these problems will solve themselves.

## Inflexibility

A fuel oil burning plant can burn fuel oil from any source so long as the physical properties are similar. If necessary, blending can easily be carried out to achieve the desired physical characteristics.

The same flexibility and relative consistency in physical properties are not available in the case of coal. Coal from one mine can differ substantially in characteristics and quality from those of coal from another mine so that a plant that is designed to burn coal from one source may not necessarily be able to burn coal from another. It is true that a plant can be designed to burn a range of coal of different qualities. This can only be achieved at the sacrifice of optimum design. To all intents and purposes, a steam plant is best designed to burn coal from one specific source.

This constraint generates the concern that a plant will be rendered inoperable should the source of coal be interrupted owing to such unforeseen factors as industrial strikes at the mine. Such a concern is valid but there are steps one can take to minimize such a risk.

Firstly, the plant can be designed to have dual fuel firing capability. In other words, normally the plant would operate on coal but could switch over to operation on fuel oil when necessary. Secondly, the boilers can be designed to accept a limited range of different coals at a small sacrifice of optimal operating conditions so that some degree of substitution could be achieved, if required. Thirdly, different stages of development of a major power station could be designed to use coal from different sources from different countries, if need be, so that should one source dry up, only part of the station will be affected.

The third precaution is particularly important as apart from diversifying the sources of supply, substitution of coal from one source for another is thus possible if care is taken to ensure that the coal qualities from the different sources do not vary too much. By having these safeguards and possibilities, coal supply would be considerably secured. Coupled with the provision for burning fuel oil as a last resort, there should be little fear that a coal-firing station would be crippled owing to the non-availability of coal from any one source.

## Pollution

The most difficult problem in using coal is to overcome the fear that a coal burning power station will result in intolerable pollution to the environment. Actually, in so far as SOX emission is concerned, a coal burning station can be cleaner than a fuel oil station. Most coals contain from 1 per cent to 1½ per cent sulphur, whereas the normal run of fuel oil contains from 2½ per cent to 3½ per cent sulphur.

The problem with coal lies in its ash content. However, with modern electrostatic dust precipitating equipment, 95 per cent or more of the ash could be precipitated. Another source of dust could come from the unloading and conveying of coal. This source of dust is confined to the vicinity of the power plant and the problem can be overcome through proper engineering design such as the provision of fine water sprays and a totally enclosed conveyor system.

A coal burning power plant need not actually be detrimental to the environment if one is prepared to invest in anti-pollution equipment. Finally, in connection with the use of coal, one question that has often been asked is whether we can burn coal in our existing power stations. The answer is no. A plant originally designed to burn coal can be converted to burn oil as has been done to many boilers in the last thirty years until the fuel oil crisis. The reverse, however, cannot be done. This is because a fuel oil burning furnace is very much smaller than a coal burning furnace for the same capacity of steam output. Additionally, there is no room in a fuel oil plant to accommodate coal storage, coal conveying, and crushing equipment as well as ash handling and disposal facilities.

**Natural Gas**

Another question that has often been asked relates to the reasons for our not using natural gas to fire our power station boilers when we are in the proximity of major gas fields. There are several reasons for this. For the gas to be used, it must be transported to the power station. Transportation of the gas can take two modes. It can be conveyed by pipeline in its gaseous form or it can be liquefied at source and transported to site as liquefied natural gas.

For transport by pipeline, the source of the gas must not be too far away from the point of utilization for economic reasons. For example, if there is a substantial gas field off the east coast of Malaysia and there is a surplus for export to Singapore, it would be feasible to envisage a gas pipeline coming down Peninsular Malaysia into Singapore. Indeed in anticipation of such a possibility the boilers at the Senoko Power Station have basic design features incorporated into them so as to enable them to accept natural gas if available. However, it would appear that the gas find off the east coast of Malaysia is not of a substantial quantity and presently the possibility of export to Singapore appears to be remote.

Natural gas from fields further away, such as those in Brunei, if it is to be used in Singapore, must be transported here in special tankers as liquefied natural gas. There must also be a special receiving terminal and storage facilities in Singapore to receive and store the liquefied gas and subsequently to reconvert it to its gaseous form for use. Because of the very low temperature involved, an LNG terminal is a very expensive installation, costing anything up to one billion dollars or even more. Such an expenditure can only be justified when a very large-scale operation is involved, which would not be so in our case.

Thus the advantage of our proximity to major gas fields is therefore more apparent than real. Moreover, the outputs of major gas fields in our vicinity are under long-term supply contract to Japan where there is a great demand for natural gas because of environmental considerations. At any rate, diversification into reliance on natural gas, even if economically viable, is strategically not advisable. Like fuel oil, natural gas is limited in availability and because it is a clean fuel competition for its use is likely to intensify and price will escalate as fast if not faster than fuel oil. In the longer term, like fuel oil, it should be conserved for feedstock for petrochemical processes rather than burning as fuel.

### Solar Energy

Sunshine is plentiful in this part of the world. It is a non-exhaustible source of energy. It is completely non-polluting. It is however not "free" as many people would like to believe. It costs money to collect the energy of the sun, to concentrate it, or to convert it to usable energy.

We may harness the heat of solar energy directly or converting it to electricity using photo-voltaic cells. The problem with using solar energy as a heat source is that it is a low-grade source of heat. In other words, the level of energy intensity per unit area is so low that we require a very large area to collect and concentrate the energy to any usable level or quantum. Without concentration solar energy is useful only for water heating purposes. These are exemplified by the flat plate collectors for hot water installations, a number of which are found in Singapore.

For solar energy to be raised to a level able to perform more useful work such as the running of an absorption cycle refrigeration or air condition plant or raising steam in a boiler, we need a large number of reflective collectors with sun tracking capability to collect and concentrate the low level energy. The implications are, firstly, we need a large area (which we do not have) to site the collectors and, secondly, the installation is very complex and expensive.

Economics also works against the use of solar energy by the process of conversion to electricity using photo-voltaic cells, except for special applications. Added to this is the problem that no electricity is generated when the sun is not shining. To overcome this a storage system is required. Based on present-day technology the storage of electricity is by means of conventional batteries which are expensive and whose capacity is at any rate fairly limited. The need for a storage system further adds substantially to the total cost of generating electricity from solar energy and detracts from its economic viability.

While solar energy is not practical nor economical to meet any substantial energy demand, it should be noted that this is an area where a great deal of research and development work is being done and the technology is developing very rapidly. Less costly methods are being found for the manufacture of silicon wafers for use in photo-voltaic cells and a whole new range of storage batteries with far superior performance is being developed.

With the price of conventional fuel escalating on the one hand, and the cost of solar equipment dropping on the other owing to new developments and large-scale manufacturing operations, the economics of solar energy could become increasingly more attractive. However, because of the inherent nature of solar energy, and especially in the light of our own conditions, it would be naive to expect solar energy to make any substantial contribution to our total energy requirements. At best, solar energy will come as a supplement to a central supply of energy from more conventional sources. Even by the turn of the century, it is not expected that solar energy will contribute anywhere near 10 per cent of our total energy requirements.

**Wind and Ocean**

Wind energy is not considered practical in Singapore. We do not have a strong prevailing wind here, and at any rate power outputs from such devices are small compared to our total energy requirements. The only possible application of wind-powered electricity generating devices is on some of our offshore islands, too distant to bring a supply of electricity to them economically.

Likewise, energy from the ocean, either in the form of tide, wave, or thermal difference, is not available to us. We do not have extremes in tide levels. The maximum tide level difference in our case is only about 3 metres, quite out of the question for any tidal power application. Similarly, we do not have any strong waves which can be harnessed for the generation of electricity nor any deep ocean to be considered for thermal difference power generation.

**Others, Including Garbage, Bio-gas, and Alcohol**

Refuse is now being used to generate electricity in the Ministry of Environment's incineration plant. The output, however, is small and accounts for only a fraction of our total requirement. It is nevertheless a source of energy which we should continue to exploit.

Bio-gas is also harnessed on a small scale from our sewerage treatment works. Apart from human waste, the waste from our pig farms could be another source of bio-gas. It could be worthwhile to look further into the more optimal generation of this supplementary source of energy, small in quantum as it may be.

The use of alcohol as a fuel either by itself or mixed with petrol to propel motor vehicles merits our attention. We do not have of course the hinterland to grow the raw material for alcohol production, but many areas in this part of the world have. We could help to develop, either by joint ventures or other arrangements, such plantations and serve as a centre for the production of this fuel.

## Power Import

Importation of power is not truly an option similar to the others that have been discussed, but it is one that we can consider. Vast hydroelectric potentials are known to exist both in Sumatra and in East Malaysia. These areas, however, require little power. It has been suggested that these hydro potentials could well be developed for the export of power to both Singapore and Malaysia. The suggestion is not without merit, though there are tremendous technical and other problems to be overcome.

For example, the transport of power from East Malaysia to Singapore will involve a submarine high voltage d.c. link over a distance far greater than anything that has ever been attempted before. In any event, for reliability and security of supply it is not possible to rely too heavily on imported power.

## Conclusion

Because Singapore has no indigenous fuel resources it has no alternative to turn to. For this reason, it is all the more important that it must create as many options as possible. No one option is likely to be able to solve our energy problems of the future. The solution seems to lie in capitalizing on a number of options at the appropriate points of time until we have a sufficiently large number of complementary sources of energy to make us reasonably secured in our supply.

To start off, energy conservation, while not strictly an energy option, should continue to be given priority. We should then work quickly to diversify our dependence on liquid petroleum products for our energy needs. For the moment coal seems to provide the best option and towards the later part of this century, we should have a reasonable portion of our electricity generating capability based on coal. Nuclear energy should not be written off entirely as it could play a part at the appropriate point of time and under the right circumstances. Concurrently, we should work towards the greater use of solar energy as a supplement to a central supply of electricity.

We should continue to exploit the production of energy from refuse, encourage the production of bio-gas where feasible, and explore the possibility of the production of alcohol. We should continue to work in close collaboration with our neighbouring countries, to help and back one another up, and where appropriate, to evolve schemes which are mutually beneficial.

# 9

## Limits to Medicine

### Wong Hock Boon

That there are limits to medicine (I use the term "medicine" to mean the art and science of that discipline) should be obvious to everyone, doctor and layman alike, as there are limits to everything, whether it be space travel or fossilized fuel. Unfortunately, the extent of these limits are often not realized by laymen as well as by doctors. This non-realization is chiefly due to the progress of medicine itself, especially in the last fifty years of our civilization, a progress which has been gigantic compared to the progress of medicine since the beginning of time, as far as human beings are concerned. This sudden acute gradient of success, unfortunately, has not been sustained, and cannot be sustained in the immediate future, and failure to realize this has dimmed the progress made and, in some instances, has caused retrogression, a sliding back. In other words, there is no doubt that in the present era of medical evolution, we are seeing the failures of medical success.

To understand health and disease in living organisms, we must have an idea of Genetic Evolution. This is a process whereby genes change or mutate as a result of cosmic rays, virus infection, and other influences. The new individual with the mutated gene is "tested" by the environment in which this new individual finds itself, so that if the mutated gene is an improvement, this new individual stands a better chance of survival and, as a result, will pass on this mutated gene to his offspring. After a long period of time, this mutated gene will "replace" the original gene just because it is a superior gene.

On the other hand, if the mutated gene is an inferior one, the new individual will have a smaller chance of survival and the gene will be lost with this individual if it proves to be lethal, or it will disappear after a few generations if it be not lethal but is inferior to the original gene. By this accidental trial and error process, natural selection takes place, that is, the environment naturally selects the best, so that if the environment remains unchanged for thousands and millions of years, a particular type of living organism can only get "better" in terms of survival with time.

Therefore, human genes have improved themselves over the ages as far as diseases are concerned, and we know that our genes have not reached the ideal state yet of protecting ourselves against disease. But what we must understand is that as human beings, natural selection has brought us to as high a protective state against disease as it is possible, in an environment which existed thousands of years ago.

This was how our genes mutated and were selected for an unchanging environment for years and years (except in times of unexpected environmental change such as the ice age, etc.). However, for these mutated genes to establish themselves and supplant the previous so-called normal genes takes thousands of years, of course. In other words, it takes a long time — for natural selection to be successful, it is not an overnight affair. This period did not matter in the old days when the environment was static, because the mutation was preparing the human being to survive better in that unchanging environment. Unfortunately for natural selection, our environment has been drastically changed in the last few hundred years because of advances in scientific technology, so that the mutated genes, ideal for the previous environment suddenly come up against a totally different environment for which they had not mutated, and against which they have not been selected (Figs. 1 and 2).

## Fig. 1 Genetic Evolution

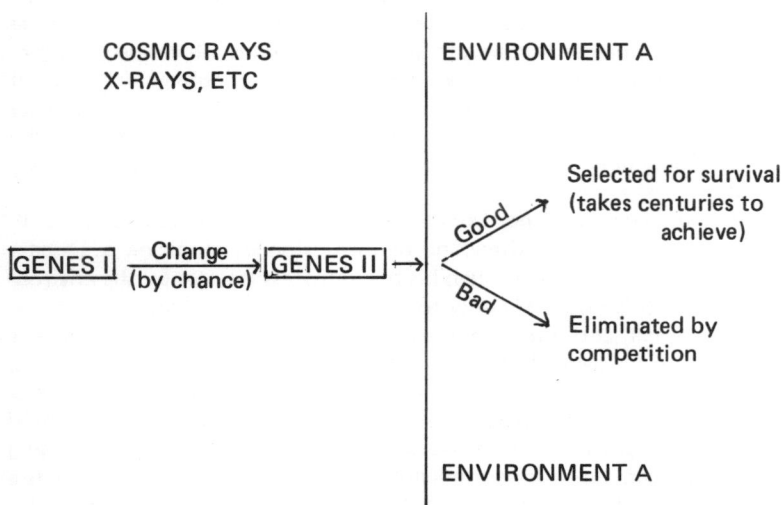

COSMIC RAYS
X-RAYS, ETC

ENVIRONMENT A

Selected for survival
(takes centuries to
achieve)

GENES I —Change (by chance)→ GENES II →

Good

Bad

Eliminated by
competition

ENVIRONMENT A

**Fig. 2  Social Evolution**

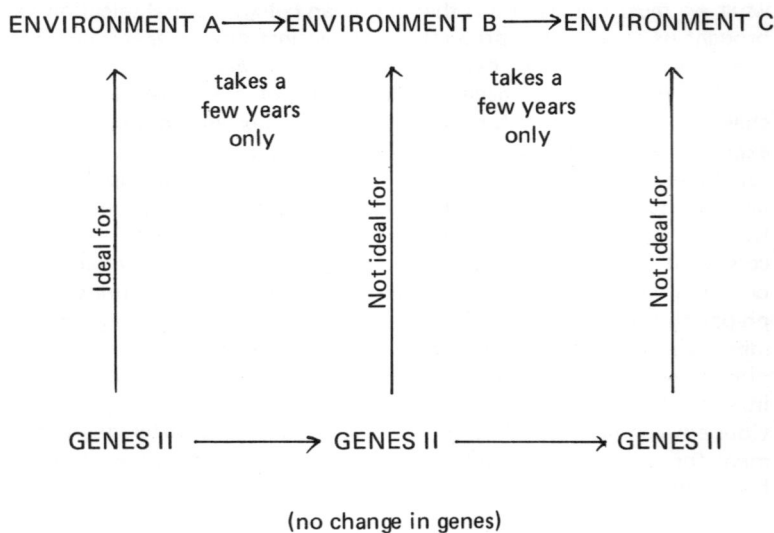

ENVIRONMENT A——→ENVIRONMENT B ——→ENVIRONMENT C

↑          takes a        ↑        takes a        ↑
           few years               few years
           only                    only

Ideal for                 Not ideal for              Not ideal for

GENES II ————→ GENES II ————————→ GENES II

(no change in genes)

If we refer to natural selection as a process acting on mutated genes and causing genetic evolution, I would like to refer to the changes which we ourselves make in our environment as Social Evolution, as this term embraces human attitudes and fashions which also conspire to change the environment besides scientific technology. After all, it is the human being making use of the progress in scientific technology which changes the environment. Social evolution is not natural in the sense that genetic evolution is natural, that is, it is artificial, it is man-made.

We are now in a position to appreciate and understand what disease is and what the discipline or profession of medicine is. Disease is a state in an individual when his body process is upset by the environment, and this refers not only to the physical state but also the mental, psychological, and other states, which are in a state of dis-ease. There is a failure of his genes to protect the individual against the environment, in spite of all his genetic evolution. It could be that he is less richly genetic-endowed, as a person suffering from schizophrenia, or it could be that the environment is overwhelming as in an accident happening to a good genetic-endowed individual. On the other hand, medicine is a man-conceived discipline trying to make a person whole again after he is dis-eased. It is thus seen that the doctor is forced to operate in a rather narrow frame as he cannot change the genes of the individual who is diseased. Let us now see how man has, through the ages, tried to deal with human diseases.

### Evolution of Medicine

From the earliest times in recorded human history, diseases were construed as being due to visitations by evil spirits, and various types of treatment, mainly ritual or ceremonial, were devised to exorcise the evil spirits. Such practices persist even today in primitive tribes, and even in modern societies, remnants of such beliefs are extant. The Chinese in Singapore still carry on some of these practices, and even today in the grounds of the Singapore General Hospital, joss sticks, candles, paper money, and infusions of Chinese herbs are scattered to drive away evil spirits or invoke good spirits to aid in the recovery of loved ones.

The medicine man of primitive societies tried different methods of getting rid of the demon. The patient may be vigorously squeezed and pummelled, beaten, starved, fumigated by evil-smelling substances, or be given nauseous medicines in the hope that he would vomit out the evil spirit. The origin of the so-called body massage with oils and herbs stems from this belief. Or the demon may be persuaded to leave the patient for a more congenial host, for example, the Vedas in India entreat the demons of jaundice to leave the yellow patient and enter a yellow bird, and the spirit causing chills and shivering with fever is persuaded to leave and enter a frog, and so on. Or the demons are forced to leave by charms and incantations usually presided over by a priest or witchdoctor. And if a witchdoctor is able to charm a demon out, could he also not cause harm by invoking a demon to inhabit a person, as in witchcraft or voodoo, and so on? The social evolution of medicine started off as a profession or trade engaged in removing disease by chasing out demons, that is, medicine based on the supernatural.

The next phase in the social evolution of medicine was the empiric observation of the effects of certain substances given orally on the disease in a patient. Most of these substances were of vegetable origin, and out of this arose the evolution of what we now call "drugs". How did man come to get this idea of oral "medicines" for illnesses? I think it arose from empirical observations of primitive man who foraged for food and ate leaves, roots, fruits, grasses, etc., by trial and error. In the process he learnt what could be food and what could be poisons, the latter producing mild symptoms or occasionally severe symptoms resulting in death. He also observed the same effects when certain animals ate these substances, and he must have studied these symptoms in both man and animals, and for animals, early man may actually have initiated animal experimentation to observe the effects of these vegetable substances. On the other side of the coin, some of these astute men may have observed beneficial effects, symptomatically, at least when some ill human beings ate these substances. In this way, the art of drug medicine arose.

Why did all this happen? This aspect of social evolution was actually based on genetic evolution — that plants being unable to move can only ensure their survival from animal predators, including man, by undergoing natural selection. In their process of accidental genetic evolution, they elaborated certain substances, which if eaten, would cause poisoning. Animals and man learn this by experience, sight, smell, memory, and they avoid these plants.

It is obvious that plants did not "provide" drugs for man on purpose. It is a totally accidental, unpremeditated happening. It is equally obvious that animals and men, over millions of years, also had genetically evolved a system whereby they could be protected against these poisons. We now know that this is so in man, and the liver and kidneys bear the brunt of all drugs taken by man. In other words, every drug taken by man which is alien to his body must stress his liver and kidneys, and this is still the "price" we have to pay for sampling drugs as primitive man sampled plants for food. It is thus seen that this second stage in the social evolution of medicine was still based on conjecture and empiricism, and not on sound scientific knowledge of the anatomy and physiology of the human body. It was ineffective medicine, and occasionally could cause harm to the patient.

The next stage in the social evolution of medicine involved the beginnings of the study of the human body, coinciding with another aspect of the social evolution of man, that is, the capacity for organizing war with weapons. Wounds of various types afforded a greater opportunity for the "doctors" of the day to observe bleeding, fractures, abdominal and other organ injuries, formation of pus, gangrene, and other pathologies. It is true that opportunities such as these had already presented themselves when accidents happened to primitive man or when he was mauled by animals he was hunting. But it was organized war that presented him with the urge to study the anatomy of man.

First, animals were slaughtered and studied, and later live patients, and dissection of the dead. The beginnings of scientific anatomy were thus firmly laid. Hippocrates, the father of Greek medicine and still revered by the present medical profession, practised medicine about 400 B.C. with some knowledge of the human body, but it was in 300 B.C. when Ptolemy I established the "Museum" of Alexandria where human dissections were displayed that human anatomy was actively studied. The attitude towards human dissections swung the other way, and it was said that the Ptolemies, in their zeal for science, handed over criminals to Herophilus and Erasistratus, two renowned anatomists, who opened the various cavities of living bodies in the hope of making important discoveries. The setting of fractures, making holes in the skull to remove clots, pus, and evil spirits were practised by Greek, Roman, and Arabic doctors. Surgery as practised had some anatomical basis but little physiological basis. It was Galen who discovered some physiological principles and tried to relate the use of certain drugs on these principles. However, we know that, like the Asian system of medicine, it was more philosophy than science.

It was during the Renaissance (1300—1450) that medicine took a further step forward when Italian workers — Leonardo da Vinci, Vesalius, and Fallopius, laid the foundation of modern anatomy and physiology. In spite of all this, medicine as practised was mainly still unscientific. William Harvey, who in 1628 published his discoveries on the heart and the circulation, and Van Leeuwenhoek, who in 1683 discovered the microscope, provided the ladder on which others after them made significant advances in medical discoveries and laid the foundation for modern scientific medicine. As with all social evolution based on science, once the groundwork had been laid, progress was rapid. In fact, scientific progress in medicine in the last fifty years outstripped its progress over the last three thousand years.

## Modern Ideas on Disease

As mentioned above, the human body had genetically evolved to protect itself against disease, but over millions of years, the perfect system has yet to be evolved. At conception the genes are already programmed to assure this rule throughout life and the genes are also programmed to allow the individual to live a certain limited life span — man is not immortal. Obviously, there are natural limits to medicine, and no matter what the doctor does, death in old age is inevitable.

But before we discuss present-day views on disease and treatment, we must remember that the process of genetic evolution to protect the organism had proceeded hand-in-hand with the environment; in fact, it had been the environment which had "channelled" this genetic evolution. But because of the change in the environment caused by man as a result of scientific technology and as a result of change in life-styles, the "protective" genes find great difficulty in performing their task in an alien environment artificially produced by man, for example, smoke pollution, cigarette smoking, the travelling vehicle, the urban jungle instead of the flora and fauna in which the genes evolved, the stress in modern life-styles, etc. This changed environment must always be in the forefront when we discuss and think about modern medicine.

Infection is still one of the main causes of disease in man. Infection in man had its genesis as early as life on earth. Besides being herbivorous, animals are also carnivorous. For life, food must be obtained. Unfortunately, except for plants, food must be obtained from other living objects. Each lives and procreates on the other. Where man is concerned, many germs have learnt to live in our bodies without causing harm — we call them commensals — especially in our throats and mouths, large intestines, and elsewhere. We tolerate them, provide a haven for them to live and multiply, and very often these organisms show their appreciation by protecting us from other predators and manufacture important substances for our sustenance. Upset of this ecology could be disastrous as in the instance of indiscriminate use of antibiotics.

Man is still in the process of trying to accommodate all organisms but has not reached that stage, and when this happens in the case of a particular organism, for example, the influenza virus, the tetanus bacillus, the tuberculous germ, etc., man becomes infected. Man is still far away from the day when he could come to terms with germs. All animals show the same phenomenon of germ adaptation — fish, rats, plants, snails. The discovery of the germ is a recent thing in the social evolution of medicine and is still not fully complete, the Legionaires Disease germ being an example. So the first big advance in modern medicine is the recognition of the germ.

The second important concept of medicine recently is the discovery of the protective system of the body which is called the Immunological System, and diseases which arise because of abnormality of this system. By a complex system of antibody formation, the immunological system of man attacks foreign substances which may invade it, including germs but not exclusively so. The immunological system of some human beings has "overdeveloped", so that antibodies are produced to substances which are tolerated by most others, for example, some are intolerant to certain foods such as the protein in cow's milk, the dust in the air for the asthmatic, certain drugs such as a shock reaction to penicillin injection, certain chemicals to the skin, and many others. This is an example of how a body system by being oversensitive or too finely honed works against the individual. It is this same system which causes problems for the doctor carrying out organ transplants, as other people's organs are foreign to the recipient except those of his identical twin, if he has one.

It is this same immunological system which we make use of in prophylactic immunizations by giving a germ which, though it has been tamed so that it cannot cause disease, is able to stimulate the production of antibodies against the disease. The BCG for tuberculosis, teta-

nus, diptheria, whooping cough, poliomyelitis, measles, and German
measles vaccinations work on this principle. This is indeed a triumph of
medical science. Again, it is this system which causes two allied diseases,
one of which is termed auto-immune disease such as diabetes where
the immunological system occasionally loses its capacity to "recognize"
his own tissues and begins to produce antibodies against them, destroy-
ing them, for example, the diabetic producing antibodies to his own
pancreas. The other disease is cancer, when the immunological system
which supervises and monitors the orderly growth of our tissue cells
suddenly fails to do so, so that a tissue cell grows wildly and produces
a cancer. Medical researchers have just realized that many diseases are
due to a failure of this immunological system, and in many instances,
medicine is powerless to deal with diseases caused by an abnormality
of this system.

The third group of diseases are produced by abnormal genes. In fact
all diseases are produced by genes which are abnormal at conception
or became abnormal with time. However, there is a group of diseases
referred to as genetic diseases where the mutated gene is at a dis-
advantage in the environment and destroys the person harbouring it.
The Mongol, the haemophiliac, and over three thousand such diseases
have been recognized, and each year new ones are added to the list.
It is in this group of diseases that medicine is relatively helpless, as
helpless as in the treatment of most cancers. The only effective method
of dealing with these diseases is by prevention.

The fourth group of diseases are mental diseases. We must realize that
the brain and its nerves, that is, the nervous system, controls not only
itself but all organs of the body. When it is activated, it releases chemicals called neurotransmitters which transmit impulses from one place
to another, and in this manner controls the growth and function
of tissues, including the blood vessels. The capacity to produce these
neurotransmitters varies from one individual to another by virtue of the
possession of different genes, and it is no surprise that no two people's
nervous system act in the same manner. Controlling all these nervous
activities are the higher centres referred to as the cerebral cortex, and
similarly, no two people's cerebral cortices function identically.

We can explain three groups of "diseases" due to some "abnormality"
of the cortex and other higher centres. The first group comprises the
mental disorders, a term covering schizophrenia, depression, and other
behavioural disorders where the neurotransmitters are disordered and
a large part of this disorderliness is due to inherited genes but often
provoked by the environment. The less severe mental disorders such as
the psychoneuroses, for example, acute anxiety, changing moods, etc.,
are also caused by a combination of genes and the environment. In
modern society, these mental disorders are more commonly recognized

because of the increasing stress in modern living and because irrational behaviour in such a stressful competitive society is less tolerated by others.

The second disorder is mental retardation, which again is due to a combination of genes and environment, so that the nervous system is less able to equip the person with sufficient capabilities highly prized by society. Such persons will always be inferior to others in day-to-day functioning, and again such persons would be more easily categorized as society becomes more complex and more competitive. The third nervous system disorder is the psychosomatic disease. As explained earlier, the brain controls all the organs and tissues, some at a conscious level (the movements of limbs) and some at a subconscious level (the heart beats, the intestinal contractions, etc.). Disorders of this type arise when a person's genes allow him to overact so that the organs suffer as a result of the nervous system's overactivity. Bronchial asthma, peptic ulcer, heart attacks, high blood pressure, thyrotoxicosis, vague aches and pains in the body — all these have a certain causative contribution made by the person's nervous system. Again, it is a combination of the genes and the environment.

The fifth group of diseases are those due to trauma, and the study of such traumatic disorders started in the earliest days of mankind has provided surgery with opportunities to try and correct the ravages caused, and in some instances save the patient's life. Not all patients with trauma can be saved; the homicide's bullet and bearing-scraper, the bus and the car, the factory machine, the fall from the high-rise flat, etc., often result in lesions which are lethal even before surgery can be attempted, or the lesions are so extensive that surgery cannot do anything at all. Diseases from trauma are not insignificant in the sum total of human morbidity and mortality as motor accidents are the greatest killers of man in his prime age in modern urban countries.

The sixth group of diseases are those which arise in a manner which I call "natural". The study of human conception, growth, and development reveals that the acme of growth and development is reached about the age of 25—30 years. After that all the tissues undergo a process of senescence and degeneration. There is no escape although the rate and degree of such senescent degenerative changes vary from individual to individual. The cataract, the hardening of the arteries, the mental deterioration, the unsteady hand, the panting breath, the loss of hair — all these have been programmed by the genes, and with slight variations are inevitable. Hence, we expect diseases to become more frequent with old age, and it is to be expected that medical science has less to offer.

The seventh group of diseases are the deficiency diseases, that is, diseases due to a deficiency of a vitamin or a hormone for which there is a replacement substance isolated by medical science. Many of these are nutritional deficiency diseases, such as mass starvation for which there is no drug except food, avitaminosis for which vitamins are available, such as blindness due to Vitamin A deficiency, beri-beri due to Vitamin B deficiency, scurvy due to Vitamin C deficiency, rickets due to Vitamin D deficiency, and so on. Yet, these same deficiencies could be prevented or cured by taking the right food. However, deficiencies include diabetes, due to lack of insulin, hypothyroidism due to lack of thyroxine, Addison's disease due to lack of cortisone, and so on. In spite of the availability of such hormones for substitution therapy, the provision of the drug is not quite the same as the natural hormone, for example, although insulin has saved many diabetics' lives, patients still die prematurely from the side-effects of diabetes.

The eighth group of diseases are the iatrogenic diseases — diseases which arise because there are doctors. Most of them are due to indiscriminate drug prescribing and their side-effects. The liver and kidneys will have to overwork to get rid of the drugs. Drug addiction is another example of a serious iatrogenic disease. It is not only doctors who are responsible but also the drug companies, many of which are large multinational companies in the business mainly for profit. Besides drugs, cows' milk preparations for babies may give rise to allergic reactions. The easy availability of drugs not only cause addiction but also accidental poisoning, as well as premeditated suicidal poisoning.

In conclusion, most of the diseases of man can be slotted into one or other, or a combination of the above eight groups. We are now in a position to assess critically the limitations of medical science as practised by most doctors to deal with the above diseases.

## Limits to Medicine in Infections

Of all the medicines to combat infections, the antimicrobials, of which the antibiotics are the prime example, have saved many lives. However, they are effective only in bacterial infections and not viral infections, for which suitable antibiotics are still not available. Unfortunately, 80—90 per cent of all infections afflicting man are caused by viruses and not bacteria. The layman, not realizing this, expects the doctor to give him an antibiotic for any fever, so that the indiscriminate use of antibiotics is extremely prevalent. If antibiotics do not produce side-effects, this practice would not be of any consequence. Unfortunately, this is not so, and upset of the ecology of the normal bacteria in our bodies by such antibiotics produce superinfections[1] so that the more antibiotics are given, the longer the fever persists. Some antibiotics cause bone marrow failure so that bleeding, anaemia, depression of ability to resist infection, and death occurs. In fact, almost any known disease can be caused by antibiotics, depending on the genetic

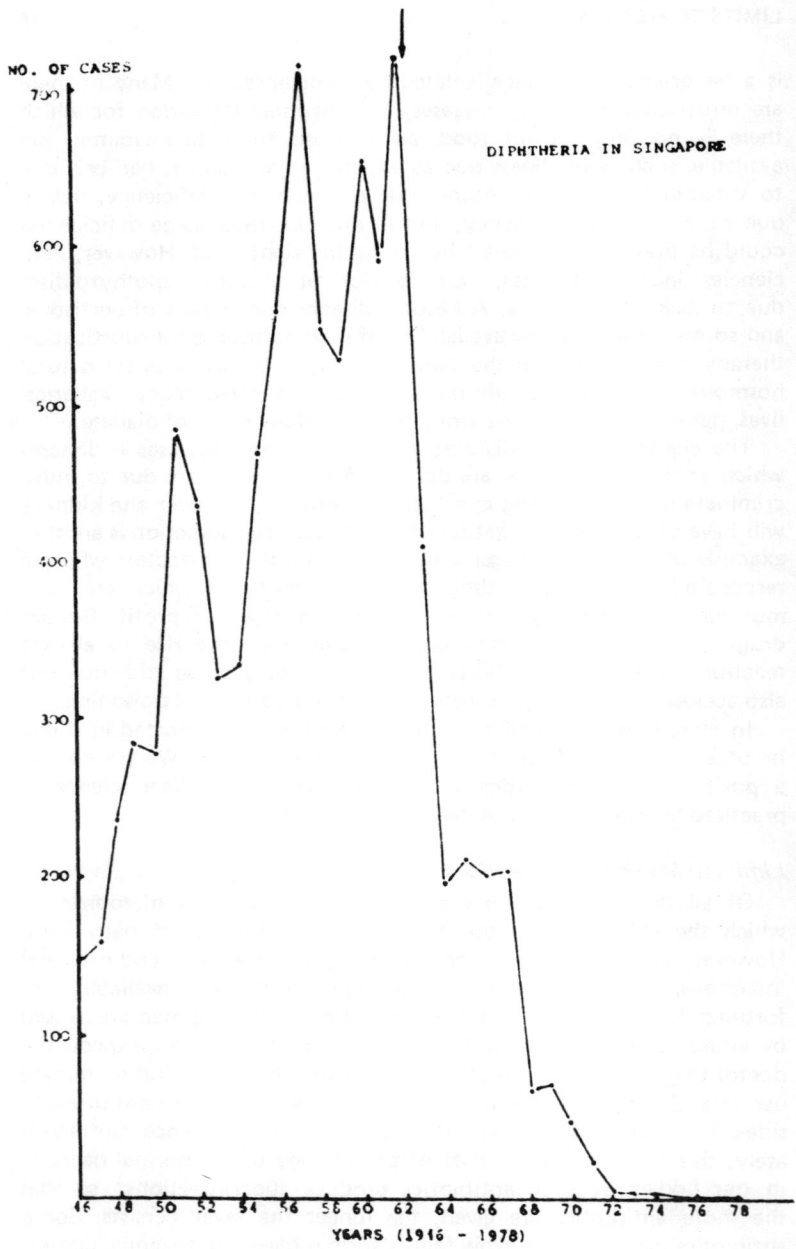

Fig. 3

susceptibility of the person, and adverse reactions to drugs severe enough to cause concern are responsible for such patients who comprise 5–10 per cent of all admissions to hospitals, and where milder cases are concerned, it is not surprising that 25–50 per cent of all illnesses are caused by drugs.[2]

Although antibiotics are effective against bacteria, the reduction in the number of deaths in patients is insignificant when compared to the efficacy of preventive inoculations. For example, diphtheria and tetanus are caused by bacteria which are sensitive to a wide variety of antibiotics which have been available in Singapore since the 1950s. Yet during this time the prevalence of diphtheria and the incidence of deaths from tetanus were still considerable. It was only with the introduction of compulsory diphtheria inoculation that diphtheria has been wiped out in Singapore (Fig. 3), and it was only with tetanus inoculation that deaths from tetanus became negligible (Table 1).

Even with the availability of many anti-tuberculosis antibiotics, the fall in tuberculosis incidence in children in Singapore to almost vanishing point is not due to these drugs but due to BCG inoculation and better nutrition and housing (Fig. 4). It was the introduction of oral polio prophylaxis that finally wiped out polio from Singapore as there are no antibiotics against the virus (Fig. 5). In bacterial infections where there is no immunizing agent available, as in pneumonia and diarrhoea, the reduction in deaths have not been as dramatic (Figs. 6 and 7).

TABLE 1

NUMBER OF DEATHS FROM TETANUS, 1960–1978

| Year | No. of Deaths | Year | No. of Deaths |
|------|---------------|------|---------------|
| 1960 | 24 | 1968 | 8 |
| 1961 | 36 | 1969 | 12 |
| 1962 | 21 | 1970 | 5 |
| 1963 | 20 | 1971 | 10 |
| 1964 | 22 | 1972 | 1 |
| 1965 | 24 | 1973 | 7 |
| 1966 | 20 | 1974 | 7 |
| 1967 | 14 | 1975 | 5 |
|      |    | 1978 | 1 |

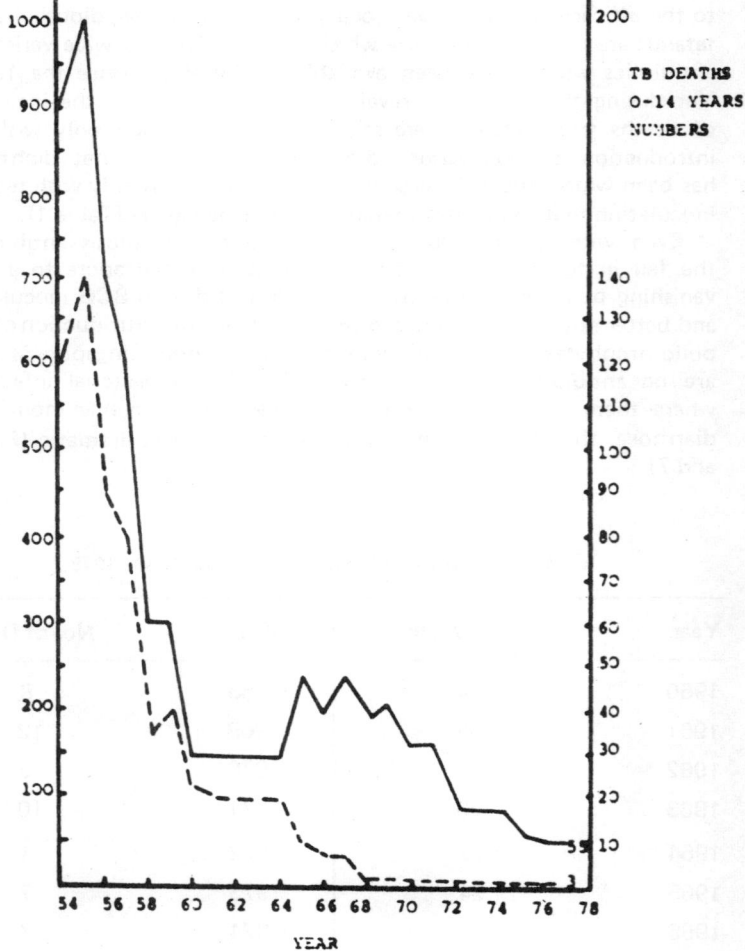

Fig. 4

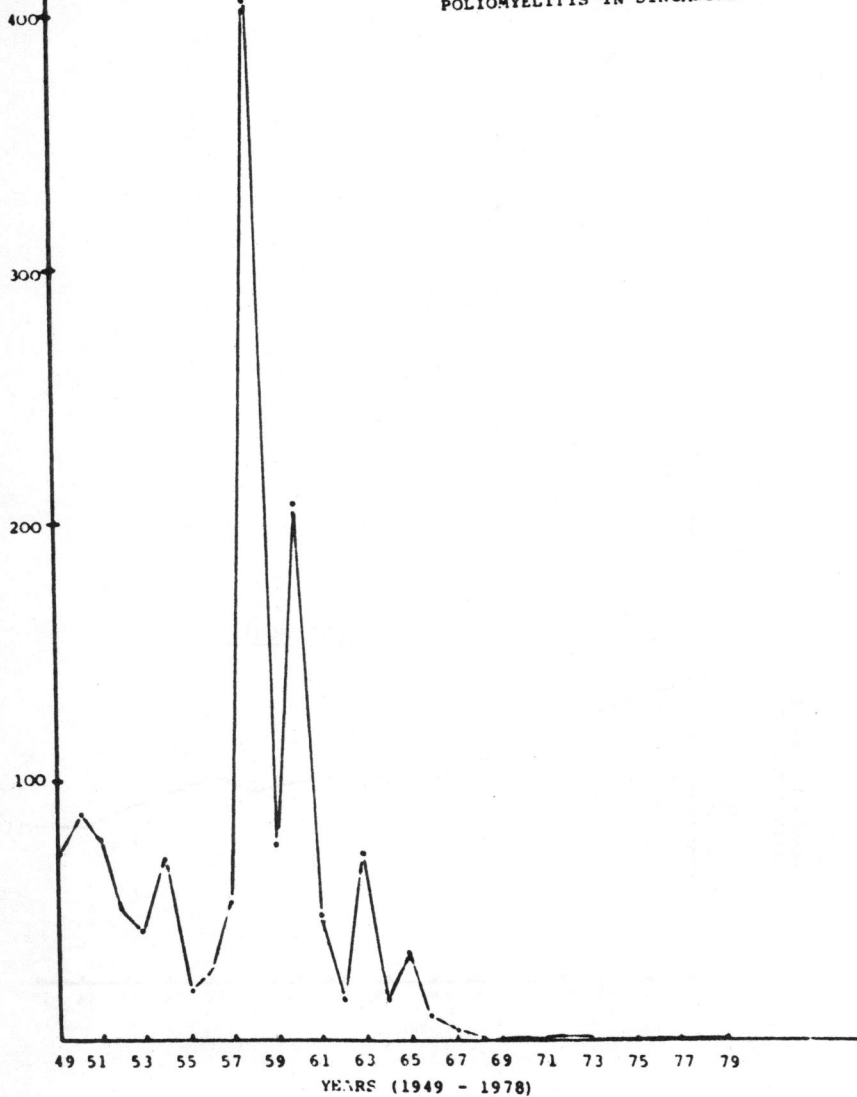

Fig. 5

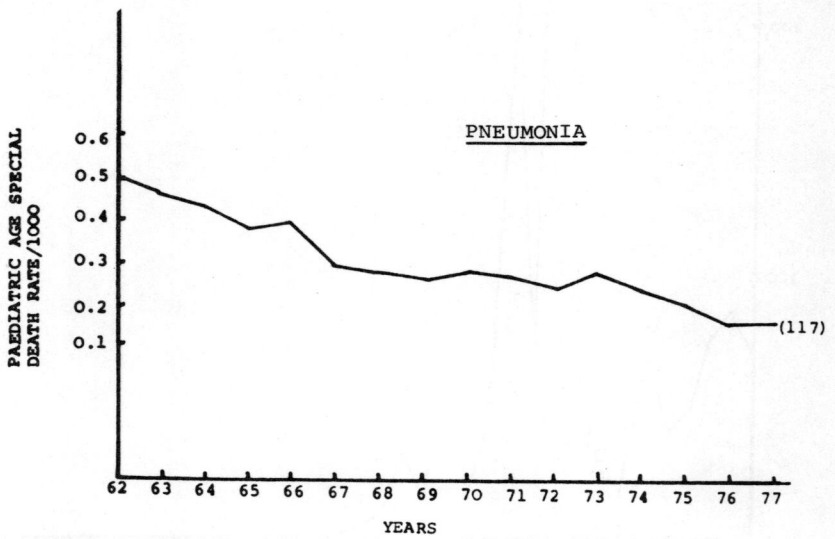

Fig. 6

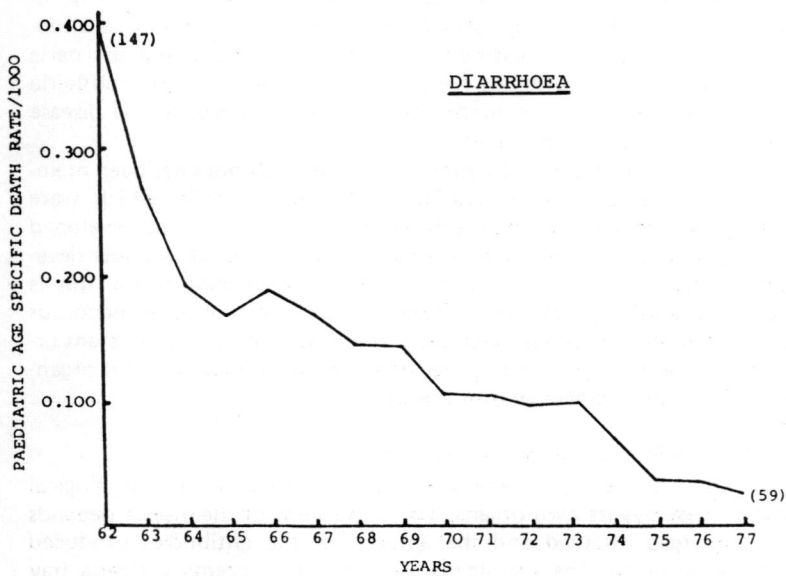

Fig. 7

It is thus seen that there are limits to the usefulness of antibiotics, the discovery of which has been acknowledged as a breakthrough in medicine, and that in future infections can be only effectively brought under control by preventive measures. In spite of available antibiotics, the incidence of gonorrhoea and syphilis has risen recently all over the world.

There is another type of limitation to the success of medicine, and that is human non-compliance. For example, although measles vaccination is effective and relatively harmless while the diseases is incapacitating and can cause death, Chinese traditional ideas have prevented the eradication of the disease from Singapore. German measles in a pregnant mother can cause mental retardation and congenital heart disease in the baby, yet many women in Singapore do not bother to inoculate themselves against German measles. Both these vaccines are available free in government clinics, and on payment of a small fee in private clinics, yet many do not avail themselves of the opportunity.

The failure of this medical success in discovering potent vaccines is due to the failure of the medical profession to educate the layman. It is also due to human nature — people are galvanized into action only when they are sick and take good health for granted. They assume that good health is a natural state, which is untrue. That is why, in medicine as in other things, occasional compulsion is the only solution. If smallpox vaccination had not been made compulsory in many parts of the world, it would not have been eradicated, and if diphtheria inoculation had not been made compulsory in Singapore, the disease could not have been eradicated.

The widespread and indiscriminate use of antibiotics has been mainly responsible for their increasing limitations. Bacteria, which were extremely sensitive to their effects, have over the years developed resistance. Staphylococcus aureus and the gonococcus have now developed resistance to penicillin, and in the case of gonorrhoea, this is causing widespread concern. Recently, a strain of pneumococcus resistant to penicillin has been discovered, and one by one, resistant organisms have emerged, and severe infections with these resistant organisms are on the increase all over the world.

## Limitations in Immunological Diseases

There are many auto-immune diseases where the immunological system destroys its own organs. The seriousness of the disease depends on the organ affected and the amount of the antibodies produced against the organ. The allergic diseases, including eczema, urticaria, hay fever, the large number of kidney diseases which result in kidney failure, some bleeding disorders, asthma, some cases of diarrhoea, and liver failure, rheumatic and rheumatoid arthritis, goitres, and other endocrine diseases, "slow virus" infections of the nervous system, some muscle paralyses — all these are caused to some extent by abnormal antibody formation due to a breakdown of the immunological system. Medicine cannot cure these diseases; it may help to ameliorate or alleviate for the time being. If a particular patient is cured, it is due to the patient's own system overcoming the deficiency.

Although we cannot cure these diseases, medical science has made use of such knowledge in organ transplantations. The greatest problem in organ transplantations is the fact that the recipient's immunological system will produce antibodies against the donor organ. Doctors therefore give powerful drugs termed cytotoxic or immunosuppressive drugs to depress the recipient's immunological system, and the consequences of this can be disastrous. Hence, severe infection can kill the patient, cancer may arise, bleeding may occur, and other organs may be damaged by the toxic drugs. Organ transplantation is an example of medical progress which has brought more problems to solve. That is why heart transplants have been given up for the time being. Kidney transplants are more successful but are by no means always successful or long-lasting. The status of cadaver donors raises social besides medical problems, and the status of live-donors equally has its social and organ compatibility problems.

Putting aside the emotional cost, the financial cost in terms of staff, facilities, equipment, and investigational tests are enormous and, of course, what is spent on organ transplantations means that less can be spent on other health measures. The limits to medicine in terms of cost-benefit ratio are realized by those who determine priorities in medical care expenditure not only in the developing countries but also in the developed countries.[3] In attempting to treat end-stage organ failure by organ transplantation, medicine produces and multiplies more diseases through their complications, and creates more problems. This can, of course, reach the stage where medical resources can run behind the delivery of health care. This is a dilemma medicine faces. Medical success begets medical failures.

### Limitations in Genetic Diseases

Disease caused by abnormal monogenic characteristics cannot be cured by medicine at the present time. Some can be tackled, for example, haemophilia. The gene for the production of a clotting factor, AHG, is deficient, and the patient bleeds spontaneously or with minimal trauma. Medical science has isolated AHG and the patient is given this by injection into his veins to provide him with this missing factor to stop the bleeding. However, this assumes that it can be given in time and patients may die or be crippled in spite of this treatment. Also, repeated injections may produce liver disease or the patient's immuno-logical system may produce antibodies to the donors' AHG, rendering it useless. Again, success brings with it other diseases. A baby with deficiency of an enzyme in the red cells, glucose-6-phosphate dehydro-genase (G6PD), may be brain-damaged at birth; however, if his condi-tion is diagnosed at birth, and care is taken not to expose him to moth-balls, herbs, and medicine, brain damage may be forestalled.[4] This is an example of how preventive measures are extremely effective in genetic diseases while therapy is impossible in most instances.

Since medicine is powerless in treating these diseases, prevention is essential. Genetic counselling is carried out in various ways, depending on the type of genetic disease.[5] Risk figures, contraception, family planning, amniocentesis, and examining the fluid and cells obtained from the fluid surrounding the foetus in the mother's uterus — all these measures can prevent the birth of a baby with a genetic disease. Because there is no effective medical treatment for most of these diseases, the baby may be mentally retarded, for example, a Mongol, but may be able to live a normal life span, which constitutes a bur-den to the family and society. If another like child is born to the family, the whole life of the parents and the family may be affected adversely. The problem in Singapore itself, just taking Mongolism as an example over eight years from 1970 to 1977,[6] reveals that more than 400 Mongols were born. Allowing for some infant deaths, the numbers born every year will swell the numbers of mental retardates in Singa-pore — and this is only one cause of mental retardation. All over the world, there are organizations or voluntary societies formed to look after the needs of mental retardates, as medical science is powerless to make them normal by treatment. Yet, it is surprising that nowhere in the world is there a society for the prevention of mental retardation operating with the same zeal and enthusiasm seen in these organiza-tions.

Of course, there are screening tests on newborns to detect certain genetic diseases. Some are useful and others are not. Those which are useful are those where certain dietary constituents may be excluded from birth and may prevent retardation. These diseases are in the minority. However, such wide-scale screening again must be subject to cost-benefit ratios, and the G6PD screening system in Singapore has proved itself cheap and extremely effective.

In conclusion, monogenic diseases show how little medicine has to offer, and illustrate clearly the limitations of medical therapy. Preventive measures can be very effective, but the fact that they have not been actively pursued by doctors and laymen demonstrates the limitation of medical education.

## Limitations in Psychological and Mental Diseases

Mental retardation has already been dealt with. The psychoses, especially schizophrenia, are not really curable. There are drugs which may supply to some extent the deficient neurotransmitters or inhibit the excess neurotransmitters. This they do after a fashion but do not cure the basic pathology and may make schizophrenics acceptable to others. Hence, prevention is extremely important.

Although schizophrenia and depressive illnesses are not monogenic diseases, their genetic inheritance is strong, and the risk to offspring before an affected child has been born and where one parent is affected is 1 in 8 to 1 in 12, and where both parents are affected it is 2 in 5, which is nearly half.[7] Therefore, steps should be taken to prevent the birth of offspring when the risk is so high, and if children are already born, to teach them a life-style with minimal stress and ways and means whereby stress may be avoided or reacted to with minimal anxiety, that is, prevent the cerebral cortex from taxing the affected neurones.

The psychosomatic diseases can be treated by medical science to some extent but mainly at the periphery, for example, in gastric ulcer disease, there are drugs which prevent excess acid formation, or the surgeon removes the ulcer and acid-bearing areas. However, we know that the acid glands are supplied by nerves which are affected by the cortex, and worry and anxiety are the usual stimulatory factors. Hence, the ability to modify the peripheral action by controlling the central headquarters is well worth cultivating not only by those with these psychosomatic diseases but by everyone.

It has been shown that relaxation techniques can lower the blood pressure in hypertensives, and similarly the ability of yogis to lower their heart rate and metabolic rate by practising this "mind over matter" technique allow themselves to be buried alive for varying periods. This is an example of how man in earliest times had discovered relaxation techniques and how such techniques have benefited their health, both mental and physical, without understanding the mechanism behind them. Now there is scientific evidence that man is capable of influencing his body for good or bad, by reacting to stress. It is the ability to remain in a relaxed state that prevents neurotransmitter upheavals which may result in psychosomatic diseases, and finally aid in their recovery.

Many doctors now believe that stress situations can affect the immunological system to such an extent that cancers can arise. We therefore see that orthodox medicine has limited itself by confining its therapeutic efforts to drugs and operations alone, in spite of the fact that medical science has proved that many psychosomatic diseases are man-made and can be prevented by the individual by training and practice. Hypertension, bronchial asthma, and even abnormal rhythms of the heart have improved by using relaxation techniques.[8] Here, it is not so much a limitation to medicine as a failure of medical doctors to take advantage of medical advances.

*Limitations to Traumatic Medicine*

In spite of the so-called advances in traumatic surgery as in the suturing back of severed fingers, hands, and noses, this is only the superficial aspect of the whole problem. We would have to look at the deaths due to trauma, that is, those who died before reaching the surgeon or died in spite of surgery. There were 201 deaths from accidents in the age group 15–35 years in Singapore in 1976.[9] The total number of deaths from all causes in the 15–35 age group was 795, so that more than 25 per cent of all deaths in Singaporeans in their prime of life was due to accidental trauma, and of course, if we add homicidal and other causes of trauma, then the incidence will be indeed higher. In the United States, where traumatic surgery is said to be relatively advanced, the percentage of deaths due to accidents and violence in 1976 (i.e., all traumatic injuries) in the age group 12–17 years was a high figure of 70 per cent.[10] The corresponding figures for all other causes of death including infections, congenital anomalies, cancers, heart disease, etc., came to only 30 per cent, so that the biggest killer was traumatic injury.

This is where limitation to medicine is seen most clearly. The paediatrician was worried about deaths from polio, diphtheria, and tetanus, and invoked medical science to discover effective prophylactic inoculations so that these diseases could be eradicated. Yet, all over the world, we seldom see traumatic surgeons making a study of the mechanics of accidents, the minds of those who cause or become the victims of accidents, and taking the lead in reducing deaths from violence. Active prevention will not only reduce deaths but will also minimize injuries so that the traumatic surgeon can produce better results. Obviously, the medical profession as a whole should get itself involved in the prevention of accidents and violence, and the medical student should be made aware of the causes of these deaths and injuries.

*Limitations to Medicine in Degenerative Conditions*

With longer life spans, the tissues of the individual get older and hence more prone to death. All organs then have to slow down their activities or carry out their activities in a less effective manner. This is evident to anyone over the age of 30–35 years, when this physical activity begins to retrogress. His heart, his lungs, his kidneys, and his eyes no longer are as "young", "sharp", or "vigorous" as before. Even if he has no other obvious disease such as diabetes or hypertension, the decay in his tissues will now give rise to symptoms.

Medical science can still assist these people but only up to a point. Drug toxicity, difficulty in repair and convalescence are so much more common. The doctor does all he can, but his efforts are limited by the substrate he is dealing with. Vigorous treatment often achieves the opposite effect, and here there is a dilemma for the medical profession to keep the patient alive at what cost. Problems in this category will loom large in Singapore in the future as more Singaporeans become senior citizens.

In fact the best way to deal with the problem is for doctors to educate the young before they become old. Good health habits in youth is a good insurance against the ravages of tissue degeneration in old age. The mind needs sustenance as much as the body, and it must be kept as active as possible. At the moment, there is no way whereby the genes can be programmed to stop or delay this degeneration.

### Limitations to Treatment of Cancer

Cancer arises because the immunological system is unable to regulate the growth of cells, and this can be further fostered by the environment as in exposure to certain environmental agents such as cigarette smoke, chemicals, drugs, irritation due to non-drainage of secretions, etc. It is also true that as a person lives longer, the immunological system becomes less effective in its surveillance role, and he has also been exposed a longer time to potential carcinogens. Hence, cancer is commoner in older people. Yet in 1976 there were 2,245 deaths from cancer in those over the age of 50 years.[11] The total number of deaths over the age of 50 years, including death due to old age, in 1976 was 8,940, so that deaths from cancer comprise 25 per cent of all deaths after the age of 50 years. There is no doubt that the incidence of cancer in Singapore is increasing. If we compare the incidence of cancer in the five-year period 1968—1972 to the five-year period after that, 1973—1977, lung cancer had increased from 1,861 to 2,587, stomach cancer from 1,635 to 1,818, liver cancer from 1,153 to 1,225, nasopharyngeal cancer from 763 to 932, cancer of the large intestine from 1,057 to 1,563, cancer of the breast from 667 to 844.[12] Now 17.6 per cent of all cancer involves the lung, 12.4 per cent involves the stomach, and 10.6 per cent involves the large intestine. The figures show that cancer is extremely common in Singapore, and its incidence is increasing, and that many of them are incurable as seen in the number of deaths. The poor success of medicine in curing cancer is a worldwide problem, and in spite of large sums of money spent in cancer treatment research, very little gains have been made — whatever gains have been made have been wiped out by the increased incidence.

Having realized its limitations, the medical profession should pay more attention to the prevention of the condition, especially dissuading the young not to take up the smoking habit. Cases of breast cancer can be reduced by inducing more mothers to breastfeed their children and more attention should be paid to getting a vaccine for the hepatitis virus in the prevention of liver cancers, and discouraging bad eating habits especially the taking of too many drugs, herbs, and excessive meats. Asians who have migrated to the United States and adopted their high meat diets are more susceptible to cancer of the bowel compared to their relatives still staying in Asia. Finally, in those cases where it is not possible to prevent cancer, then it should be detected as early as possible so as to give the best chance for survival with wide excision by surgery, deep X-ray, and drugs.

## Limitations with Iatrogenic Diseases

Medicine can cure diseases and it can cause diseases. The role of anti-biotics in causing disease has already been discussed earlier. Any drug will have its side-effect which may be minimal or severe, so that the taking of a drug must be weighed against its possible benefit or side-effect. There is no pill for every ill.

Doctors by their pronouncements can also cause iatrogenic disease, for example, in Shiraz in Iran, 476 children were diagnosed as having heart disease.[13] However, after examination at a cardiac centre, it was found that 290 were healthy, that is, 61 per cent were labelled with a disease affecting the heart, with unnecessary physical restriction and causing anxiety to the parents. In fact, 80 per cent of these healthy children were being treated by the doctors for heart disease with drugs! The sad situation was that investigations revealed that such cardiac non-disease was commoner in communities with more doctors and with more sophisticated facilities than in areas with fewer doctors and facilities. Another way whereby iatrogenic diseases are created is through the widespread use of laboratory tests, whether indicated or not, in the hope of landing a fish after casting as wide a net as possible. Because "abnormalities" in laboratory tests are usually defined as values which fall two standard deviations from the mean, 5 per cent of an ordinary population will show "abnormal" results on any single test for statistical reasons alone. The more tests performed on healthy subjects, the more likely is the discovery of "abnormal" results.

The number of iatrogenic diseases increases year by year. A book published on diseases of medical progress, that is, iatrogenic diseases caused by medical progress, first appeared in 1959 and contained 131 pages. The second edition in 1964 had 543 pages, and the third in 1969 had 925 pages.[14] It is obvious that iatrogenic diseases are increasing and not decreasing.

## Conclusion

Medicine as an art and as a science has made immense progress over the ages from superstition to more solid ground. However, it has concentrated too much in attempts to cure diseases, many of which are "incurable" within the realm of medicine. It is salubrious for doctors to recognize this, and in these instances concentrate more on their prevention. It is time for doctors to concentrate more on health than on disease, and Schools of Medicine should be changed to Schools of Health. In old China, it was said that the doctor was paid a sum by families when the members were healthy but once anyone fell sick, the payment stopped. When the patient recovered, the payment was resumed. The time is not ripe yet for such a drastic change in attitudes, but such a practice may gain acceptance in the future.

## NOTES

1. H.B. Wong, "Antibiotic Misuse in Paediatric Practice", *Journal of the Singapore Paediatric Society* 17, no. 20 (1975).

2. N. Harwitz and O.C. Wade, "Intensive Hospital Monitoring of Adverse Reaction to Drugs", *British Medical Journal* 1, no. 531 (1969); L.G. Seidl, G.F. Thornton, J.W. Smith, and L.E. Claff, "Studies on the Epidemiology of Adverse Drug Reactions", *Bulletin of Johns Hopkins Hospital* 119, no. 299 (1966).

3. R.A. Mustard, "The Case of Health", *Surgery* 80, no. 283 (1976); H. Mahler, "Tomorrow's Medicine and Tomorrow's Doctors", *WHO Chronicle* 31, no. 60 (1977); T. Cooper, "In the Public Interest", *New England Journal of Medicine* 300, no. 1185; H.B. Wong, "Medical Schools, Interdisciplinarity and Delivery of Health Care in South-East Asia", *1977 ASAIHL Lecture*, University of San Carlos Press, Cebu, Philippines.

4. H.B. Wong, "Singapore Kernicterus: The Position in 1965", *Journal of the Singapore Paediatric Society* 7, no. 35 (1965); H.B. Wong "A Surveillance System to Prevent Kernicterus in Singapore Infants", *Journal of the Singapore Paediatric Society* 17, no. 1 (1975).

5. H.B. Wong and T.S. Chua, "Genetics for the General Practitioner", *Asian Journal of Paediatrics, Obstetrics and Gynaecology* 6, no. 41 (1975).

6. H.B. Wong, "The Significance of Human Chromosome Abnormalities in Singapore", *Singapore Medical Journal* 20, no. 363 (1979).

7. H.B. Wong, "Inheritance of Schizophrenia", *SMA Newsletter,* 1979, p. 10.

8. "Learnt Voluntary Control of Heart Rate and Rhythm", *British Medical Journal* 1, no. 1491 (1977); T. Pickering and G. Gorham, "Learnt Heart-rate Control by a Patient with a Ventricular Parasystolic Rhythm", Lancet 1, no. 252 (1975).

9. *Report on Registration of Births, Deaths, and Marriages, Singapore,* 1976.

10. M.G. Kovar, "Some Indicators of Health-related Behaviour among Adolescents in the United States", *Public Health Reports* 94, no. 109 (1979).

11. *Report on Registration of Births, Deaths, and Marriages, Singapore,* 1976.

12. *Report of Singapore Cancer Registry,* University Department of Pathology, 1979.

13. B. Toorabahi, "The Emergence of Cardiac Nondisease in Children of Iran", *Israel Journal of Medical Sciences* 15, no. 202 (1979).

14. R.H. Moser, *Diseases of Medical Progress,* 3rd ed. (Springfield: C.C. Thomas, 1969).

# 10

## Whither the Fine Arts?

**Chia Wai Hon**

A friend jokingly remarked that I should change the title of this paper to "Wither the Fine Arts". In other words, perish the fine arts for all the "muck" being served up in the name of "Modern Art". My friend has a very fixed concept of what art should be. He would like to see a highly realistic art form retained for all time. He is not alone in his choice. There are many of his kind around who would prefer a retention or revival of an academic art form that dates back to pre-Impressionism. For these people, any change away from realism is anathema. In all other things — cars, furniture, interior decor, fashion, electronic goods, etc. — they would demand the latest in design, but not for the fine arts. Will this nostalgia for realism be perpetuated and carried into the year 2000? In it lies the answer to the direction the fine arts will take. Singaporeans are hard-headed pragmatists who swear by the graphs and charts. It would therefore be reasonable to assume that the form and content of the fine arts would reflect this down-to-earth outlook. Art for art's sake could only be an artistic dream. The visionary would remain a stranger in the Singapore art world.

Painting had been the dominating art activity in the past just as it is today, and will continue to be so in the foreseeable future. My discussion will therefore be concentrated around this area, with reference to the other art forms as and when there are occasions to call attention to them. On a non-participatory level, and for purpose of investment, ceramics especially Chinese pottery and porcelain would outstrip painting as the favourite item of collectors.

Sculpture, despite a need for it to enhance our public buildings and parks, is still very much neglected, although I can see a bright future for it. Commercial graphics have made tremendous advances since the days of the slick cinema posters. It has now permeated through every facet of the commercial and advertising world. Packaging design has become a way of life as manufacturers fight for survival to come up with attractive wrappings to lure consumers to buy their goods. Prints are actively promoted, though printmaking is hardly practised.

*Early Beginnings*

The future starts with the present, and one cannot talk about the present without bringing up the past. So before we can begin to speculate on what the future portends for the fine arts we need to take stock of what has happened in the past and what is happening now, and to deduce from this the shape of things to come.

The art history of Singapore is of recent origin. In the absence of record I would place the awakening of interest in the fine arts as we know it today to be around 1935, the year the Society of Chinese Artists was founded. Except for the war years, 1942—45, this Society has been active since its founding. In 1938, the Nanyang Academy of Fine Arts was started by Lim Hak Tai. It was, and still is, the only art school in Singapore that provides a foundation for the practice of the fine arts. Most of our painters today have, at one time or another, been associated with the School, either as a teacher or a student.

During these early years, scattered interest in the fine arts was maintained by the occasional exhibitions at the Chinese Chamber of Commerce or the Victoria Memorial Hall. The highlight of the pre-war years was the big retrospective exhibition of Xu Bei-Hong, the very well-known Chinese painter of horses. The post-war years were memorable for the water-colours of the Penang artist Yong Mun Sen. I mention these to show that even at this early stage there was an appetite for the fine arts, especially among the Chinese-speaking community. Other ethnic-based art societies like the Malay Art Society and the Indian Fine Arts Society were also actively promoting their own culture. The organization of exhibitions by artists from Hong Kong and China was mainly undertaken by the Society of Chinese Artists and sponsored by Chinese businessmen. Government support was non-existent.

In 1949, Dr. Gibson-Hill, who was then in charge of the Raffles Museum and Library, met Richard Walker, the Superintendent of Art for Singapore schools, and a few others to form the Singapore Art Society. The aim was to encourage and foster the practice and appreciation of the arts in Singapore. Founder members also included representatives from the various ethnic-based cultural bodies. Membership of the Society was open to all, regardless of race or creed. This multiracial art society was soon looked upon as representing the interest of the Singapore and Malayan artist. There was free intermingling of artists in the two countries, and Frank Sullivan was their unofficial spokesman. The Singapore Art Society was truly performing the duties presently taken over by the National Museum Art Gallery.

In the schools a start at organized art training was begun as early as 1923 with the appointment of Richard Walker as art master for Government English schools.[1] He was in sole charge of the art programmes for all schools till his retirement around 1950. His dedicated service to art has inspired many of his students to take up the subject as a life-long study or hobby. The Chinese schools were well looked after by a group of professional artists which included Liu Kang, Chen Wen Hsi, Cheong Soo Pieng, and Chen Chong Swee. The same group was responsible for providing the art training at the Nanyang Academy of Fine Arts. Cheong Soo Pieng in particular was the idol of many art students. His style of painting was closely followed and imitated by young aspiring artists on both sides of the Causeway. In 1968, the Baharuddin Vocational Institute was started to provide training in the Applied Arts.

At the tertiary level, the University of Malaya Art Museum was established in 1955. This was meant to be a teaching museum for students taking courses in the History of Art. The Museum Collection provided the students with "an opportunity for direct contact with original works of art and to form the nucleus of a centre for the study of art and archaeology of Southeast Asia".[2] The University of Malaya ceased to function in the Bukit Timah campus in 1962. The Museum Collection was accordingly divided equally between the University of Singapore and the University of Malaya. Lack of student enrolment for the History of Art course at the University of Singapore forced it to close in 1973. The Singapore share of the Museum Collection was transferred to the National Museum.

*Art in the Seventies*

There was an increase in art activities in the early seventies. The Ministry of Culture took the lead in organizing exhibitions not for the favoured few but for the masses. Its "Art for Everyone" series went the rounds of the community centres to give exposure to those who would not normally visit art exhibitions. It was hoped that this would generate enough interest for them to want to take up art as a worthwhile hobby. The exhibitions were primarily aimed at youngsters to help keep them off the streets and their minds off drugs. It was a praiseworthy effort that had the backing of the various art societies. The Ministry further consolidated its efforts to bring art to the people by presenting annually its National Day Art Exhibitions. The more experienced and knowledgeable members of the artistic community may find this somewhat trite, but there is no denying that the exhibitions did serve the purpose for which they were intended — to provide for an art form that could be appreciated by the uninitiated. It was the base that needed building up. The more aesthetically inclined could find their own way to strengthen areas of weaknesses as they could self-motivate themselves. They were of course equally deserving of government support and sponsorship, but those who have less were more deserving of whatever limited funds available.

So it was that much criticism was levelled at governmental quarters for its lethargy and lack of support of the fine arts.

Left to their own devices our artists showed initiative in promoting what they really believed in. Youthful impatience with accepted art concepts combined with enthusiasm for what was new resulted in the formation of the Modern Art Society in 1964. The Society believed in a revolutionary approach to painting as expounded by the Western Abstract and Action painters. Not for them the photographic realism of the camera, the picturesque postcard views of Singapore River, or the idyllic *kampong* scene. The members were for an art of the spirit, of spontaneous reaction to felt phenomena expressed in terms of the materials that one is using.

Whatever may be its shortcomings, the Modern Art Society had the conviction of its belief behind it. Annually its members presented that which they believed to be the significant art forms for a modern society. The fact that these were not usually accepted did not deter them. Just as the Modern Art Society was throwing overboard accepted art values, the Singapore Water Colour Society was committed to a back-to-nature call. Started in 1970, the Society's aim was to stop the swing to abstraction and non-figurative work, and to uphold the traditional time-tested approach. Its members believed that water colour was the most suitable medium for the Eastern artist because of its affinity with Chinese brush painting. To its credit, the Singapore Water Colour Society has produced some very skilful water colour artists today.

The Alpha Gallery is a well-run private art gallery that promotes the works of established masters, both local and foreign, as well as the young *avant garde.* It held its Inaugural Exhibition in October 1971. It is a gallery managed by artists for artists. Exhibitions are but a part of its activities. It has a core of its own regular exhibiting artists who share a common studio a few doors away, and who are prepared to meet anyone wishing to discuss art. The Alpha group holds regular sessions with visiting artists. Its list of past shows reads like a Who's Who in the Singapore art world. Its policy is to promote whatever is worth promoting. An example is the work of the primitive painters of Bali.

The highlight of the seventies was the opening of the long-awaited National Museum Art Gallery in August 1976. This ushered in a new era. The fine arts was finally given its proper status and accorded the respectability which was long its due. Exhibitions increased in frequency and variety. Besides paintings, there were exhibitions of French, Australian, and local photography, ceramics and sculpture of America, art and crafts from the Democratic People's Republic of Korea, and graphic art shows from Holland, Finland, Switzerland, and Germany. This cosmopolitan outlook on the visual arts continues to be a feature of current art shows at the Museum Art Gallery.

Of great importance towards shaping the accepted role of the National Museum Art Gallery as "a vital centre for the enjoyment and understanding of the art of the region" was the work of the Museum Education Service.[3] This unit was, and still is, responsible for a hive of activities that catered to the very young right through to the school leavers. Its Young People's Gallery shared equal responsibility with its adult counterpart in developing the aesthetic sensibilities of young minds towards an appreciation of the arts.

## Towards the Year 2000

As can be seen from what has been discussed, the progress of the arts over the years has been very slow. Singapore, as it moves towards the year 2000, will not see any dramatic changes in the fine arts. The slow tempo started in the early years will be maintained and slightly accelerated. However, there will be none of the rapid and spectacular changes that are daily transforming the city into the dynamic metropolis of the twenty-first century. Despite all that has happened since 1935, the fine arts in Singapore is just getting off the ground. The seventies was a period of consolidation. The establishment of the National Museum Art Gallery marked the beginning of a new era. The making of the Singaporean as a man of culture has begun.

With the modest start achieved since its formation, the National Museum Art Gallery should have no difficulty in building on this foundation. The Gallery stands as an affirmation of the faith that the Government places on the fine arts. This is reassuring to local artists who have for years lamented the lack of interest of those in authority. They can now concentrate on their creative activities without having to worry too much about getting a place to show their work. There is also the incentive for them to work much harder to improve in order to qualify for the privilege of showing their works in such a prestigious place. It would not be amiss, therefore, to expect much higher quality work in the near future than what is available today. A greater variety of styles and media could also be in the offing if the Museum Gallery could live up to its role as catalyst for the fine arts.

Presently in its permanent collection the Museum Gallery has 115 paintings donated by the late Dato Loke Wan Tho, 45 oil portraits of former Governors of Singapore and other historical personalities, 29 paintings and 4 sculptures by Singaporean, Malaysian, Indonesian, and other artists, and about 80 Chinese paintings. A very modest beginning indeed! The Gallery will have to build up its permanent collection. Its programme to promote and disseminate knowledge on the work of promising and talented artists in the region will come to nought if the pictures are not forthcoming. There is an acquisition vote but this is far from adequate, especially when prices of art work have escalated so rapidly in the last few years.

Like museums everywhere, there will have to be dependence on donations and bequests to expand the collection. In Singapore this may not work so well because collectors of pictures are rare. We do have collectors of Chinese paintings and artefacts, but we lack those of the stature of the Guggenheims, the Rockefellers, or the Amro Bank of Amsterdam. How then can we add to what we have? Appealing to artists for donations is the present practice. Understandably, there is a limit to what one can get from this. The artist who has given once would not be too ready to part with his work a second time, even though it may be a great honour to be asked again. The artists rightly expect the Museum Gallery to give its support by buying their work. The Museum with its very limited vote can do that much and no more. It is the big corporations and industrialists who could channel some of their profits towards the acquisition of art work. The Government could encourage this practice by granting tax exemptions on art gifts to the Museum Gallery, just as it gave tax concessions to companies that set up pioneer industries in Jurong some years back.

With the increase in wealth and leisure, the buying public for art work would be proportionately increased. The Museum and private art galleries could help generate interest in private ownership of works of art by cooperating with artists to offer picture loan services whereby pictures/art objects are rented out for a fee. If the borrower likes a picture so much that he wants to keep it, he could pay the difference in the paid-up loan fees and the actual price of the painting to gain full possession. This practice is known to be successful in the United States and is worth a try here. Given proper guidance and encouragement, this could well be the trend in art collecting in the decades ahead.

But before this situation can come about, the public must be educated in art appreciation. Research programmes must be instituted. The Museum Gallery is presently busy documenting its collection and preparing information sheets on local artists and their work. The press is bravely struggling to provide some form of art criticism and is devoting more and more space to the fine arts. Radio and television are giving good coverage to art programmes. The artistic climate has never been so conducive to growth as it is today. If this can be properly nurtured and maintained, the future for the fine arts is assured. Before the year 2000 the revamped Nanyang Academy of Fine Arts should attain the status of a national art school, and there would be a need to revive the faculty of fine arts in the University of Singapore.

Public interest in the fine arts has picked up considerably, but the same cannot be said of the schools. This is in contradiction to the fine showing of our school children in overseas exhibitions and competitions, and the enthusiastic attendance at Singapore Youth Festival Exhibitions. The talented few nurtured by enthusiastic art teachers do not give a true picture of what is actually happening in the schools' art programme. Far too many schools treat the subject as peripheral and look upon it with benign disinterest. The pressure from other more "important" subjects also helps to push it further away from the core of compulsory subjects needed for the all-round development of the child. The new Education System does provide the underachievers in academic subjects with opportunities to pursue an art course at the Baharuddin Vocational Institute if they are so inclined. The high-flyers have very little exposure to the fine arts no matter how great their interest.

The task of the art educator in the next decade or so will be to seek out ways and means to correlate art with the other subjects in the curriculum. Art on its own will not have the relevance that it would have for the schools if it were to be related with the sciences, literature, or the technical subjects. Integration would enhance its usefulness as a school subject. I believe principals would be more willing to allot it the time it deserves if they could see its supportive role and its link with the other subjects on the curriculum. This attempt at marrying the fine arts with the sciences and the humanities should occupy the attention of art teachers in the years ahead. It has to be this way to stop the practice that has started with some schools doing away with the subject at upper secondary level and cutting down on art time for the lower secondary classes.

The practising Singapore artist may not need to consider the utilitarian aspect of art but he certainly has to be more alive to his environment. His art forms should belong more to this age than what was in vogue a century ago. The harping back to a nostalgic past and a delving into one's own culture for inspiration is both inevitable and highly desirable. However, in the context of the present and the future this would be more appropriate if he could translate his feelings and observations in terms of modern advancement made in science and technology. There is a whole new world of modern equipment and materials to be explored. Each of these is capable of imagery hitherto unattainable with the conventional paint and brush method. Our artists, if they claim to be sensitive individuals, and which they are, should be adventurous enough to take up the challenge. Already there are signs that a few of the younger set are beginning to make tentative probes with plastic, acrylic paints, ciment fondu, metaform, and other mixed media. This spirit of enquiry is what is needed to revitalize the fine arts. More, I predict, will follow in their footsteps.

When concentration on subject matter is thoroughly fused with the inner conflict of the mind and the media and tools of self-expression, then we can say that we have arrived in the modern age, artistically speaking. Retention of old values and concepts in art may have senti-mental associations for many, but it will retard growth in creative thinking. A dynamic nation needs a dynamic art form that reflects its aspirations. Hanging on to past achievements is not that preferred art form.

The Government has always adopted an open-door policy where the fine arts are concerned. There is no restriction on what an artist can or cannot paint. Although a Singapore identity has been encouraged from time to time, there is no attempt to lay down rules. It has been acknowledged that it will take time to establish a distinct Singapore identity. Any attempt to push this will only result in superficiality of artistic expression. Given time and a conducive atmosphere, and the freedom to be themselves, our artists will come up with a style that will be distinctly Singaporean. The present time, and into the next decade or so, is the period of gestation. In twenty years' time it is possible that characteristics attributable to a Singapore identity may be traced in the work of our artists.

Singapore has kept abreast with the latest in scientific and technolo-gical know-how. In the field of commerce and high finance, the most sophisticated of modern equipment and techniques are used in con-ducting business. As a modern state it has all the trappings that make it tick. It is forward-looking in all fields except in the fine arts where ideas generated half a century ago are still very much the norm by which painting is judged. With constant exposure to more modern art forms, a change in attitude will come about. By the year 2000, the fifty-year gap in viewing habit should be considerably reduced.

This has not been a rosy picture. Neither has it been discouraging. If expectations as spelt out can in any way help to resolve some of the problems, this crystal-ball gazing would have been worth the effort.

NOTES

1. Richard Walker, "Ruminations," *Singapore Art Society Souvenir Magazine,* 1969.

2. "Collection of Art of the University of Singapore," *National Museum Art Gallery Official Opening Catalogue,* 1976.

3. "National Museum Art Gallery", *National Museum Art Gallery Official Opening Catalogue,* 1976.

# 11

## Cultural Change and Social Values

### Ho Wing Meng

Those of us who have witnessed the rapid and far-reaching changes that transformed Singapore from a traditional entrepot centre to what is now a bustling financial, servicing, and manufacturing economy since 1959 will realize that the increasing prosperity and success of Singapore's economy over the past twenty years have not been achieved without some of the attendant social, economic, and even political upheavals which normally sweep through societies in a state of transition.

We have been fortunate, however, that although the impact of Western technology as well as Western lifestyles and values have, to a very large extent, altered the systems of values and traditions of the people (such as the steady erosion of the concept of an extended family, the different attitude of the younger generation to the institution of marriage, the abandonment of the traditional Asian attitude of respect and filial piety for one's aged parents, a certain slackening of work ethic, job-hopping and an obsessive preoccupation with material pursuits), modernization has not produced counter reactions of a violent and revolutionary nature. Undoubtedly there have been lots of grouses, grumblings, unhappiness, and reluctant adjustments made here and there, but there have been no backlashes, no boomerangs of the sort that we read about in countries such as Iran, where some conservative and religious groups of people, deeply offended by the rapid pace of change and, particularly, the adoption of Western lifestyles and values which came with Western technology, have openly repudiated what they felt were alien to traditional Iranian culture, and led the country in revolt against the Shah and his former government.

The consequences have been disastrous, judging by recent reports of widespread violence, rebellions, frequent changes of government, and disruptions to the economy following the new wave of religious fanaticism in the country. Such is the price that some countries are willing to pay in their attempts to repudiate the effects of modernization through Western technology.

While the Singapore experience in modernization through industrialization did not result in the catastrophes that Iran faces today, we had our fair share of social, political, and economic convulsions. Indeed between 1959, when the People's Action Party (PAP) won the first general election and formed a fully elected government, and 1969, Singapore went through a turbulent decade marked by widespread industrial unrest in the form of wildcat strikes, lockouts, student riots instigated by communist-inspired trade unionists, anti-colonial campaigns, bickerings between various political parties, mounting unemployment, and a declining economy. In 1963 Singapore joined Malaya, North Borneo, and Sarawak to form a federation known as Malaysia; but that political union for us was short-lived and in 1965 Singapore abruptly seceded from Malaysia to become an independent nation.

However, political independence for a minuscule city-state posed serious problems, not the least of which was our economic viability. As a matter of fact, there were quite a few people at the time who confidently predicted that Singapore's attempt in nationhood would very soon come to grief. This is because, in their opinion, the separation from Malaysia would, among other things, result in the loss of the market which the Republic badly needed for its fledgling manufacturing industries, while the dimunitive land area, virtually bereft of natural resources and peopled by a burgeoning population of 1.5 million which was increasing at the alarming rate of between 3 per cent and 4 per cent annually, would strain the ingenuity and organizational ability of any government to the breaking point. Undaunted by these overwhelming odds, the PAP Government got down to work, and within a few years the economy was making steady progress.

Except for the unexpected decision of the British Government under Harold Wilson in 1968 to close down all Britain's military establishments in Singapore and withdraw its armed forces — a move which could have resulted in the loss of fifty thousand jobs for Singaporeans, as well as the creation of a power vacuum in this region — we have not looked back ever since, as the economy continues to register a steady growth rate of between 8 per cent and 15 per cent. Even the pause between 1974 and 1976 caused by the oil crisis failed to undo the economic prosperity and momentum of industrial development in the Republic. The story of Singapore thus far is that of a successful developing country in a state of transition, poised to meet the challenges of the next twenty years with the characteristic verve and confidence of a young nation.

Having outlined rather briefly the major events which led to the development of modern Singapore during the last twenty eventful years of its short history, we will now go on to discuss a few of the more significant social and cultural changes which have taken place and attempt, on the basis of our knowledge of existing trends, to conjecture what the future has in store for us. But before we do that, I want to make a few pertinent remarks about the application of the science of futuristics (or "futurology" as it is sometimes called) for forecasting events and social phenomena which are more straightforwardly quanti-fiable especially when they occur in inquiries peculiar to the social sciences.

Now if we were asked to make predictions concerning some parti-cular phenomena on the basis of our knowledge of existing trends in, say, the distribution and utilization of manpower, the effects of an educational policy giving greater emphasis on technical training, the impact of higher technology and automation on more effective utiliza-tion of labour resources, or the effect of continued economic growth on per capita income in 1990, since we have the expertise and data concerning these various fields of inquiry, the task is relatively easy. Among other things, we need to know certain prevailing trends, the crucial factors which make for changes in existing trends of the pheno-menon in question, and then extrapolate on the assumption that the future will be like the past, with certain modifications thrown in where necessary. For example, we know that Singapore has a popu-lation of 2.3 million people and that its annual birth rate is 2 per cent. Assuming that the rate of population growth will remain unchanged for the foreseeable future, we can determine exponentially that our population will double itself in thirty-five years. On the other hand, if our population is growing at the rate of 3 per cent annually and this rate is likely to remain so for some time, we can expect that by the year 2000 (or twenty years from now) we will have a population of 4.6 million, and so on. More generally, as long as the crucial factors determining the patterns of certain social and economic phenomena continue to obtain, or provided we can control or anticipate the kinds of changes in the variables influencing the development of some pheno-mena, the prospects of our predictions going awry are remote.

None the less, the fact remains that trends are not immutable, so that even the most carefully calculated predictions have been falsified by some totally unexpected turn of events. For example, until the major Arab oil-producing countries decided to shut off the supply of oil to the United States and many other industrial countries in Europe during the Arab-Israeli War of 1973 and then forced the price of crude oil to rise four times their previous level, who could have foreseen the enormous power and influence that the countries of the Organization of Petroleum Exporting Countries wield today? Similarly, until about a year ago who, among the most informed experts on Iranian affairs, could have foreseen that the supremely powerful Shah of Iran with his fabulous wealth would have to flee for his life and surrender the reins of his government to a little-known Muslim theologian called "the Ayatollah Rhuholla Khomeini"?

If the predictions of relatively easy-to-quantify phenomena sometimes go wrong, forecasting events and phenomena of the types which are by their very nature difficult to quantify will necessarily give more trouble. Thus if we are called upon to say what kinds of social values and lifestyles the newer generations of Singaporeans are likely to adopt twenty years from now (this being the theme of this chapter) we would soon realize that even if we were familiar with the social, economic, and political conditions of the time which engendered the kind of social values and lifestyles that Singaporeans adopt today, predicting future trends about such matters is fraught with uncertainties. This is not because we cannot devise some sort of mathematical or statistical method for quantifying people's attitudes, propensities, or aversions with respect to, say, the institution of marriage, having children, divorce, the break-up of the tradition of extended family, the care (or neglect) of the old and infirm, or even the reasons why people have become more grasping and materialistic these days, and so on. Indeed we can, and sociologists do, attempt to measure people's attitudes and reactions to these things. The difficulties and uncertainties concern, rather, attempts to predict future trends in lifestyles, in attitudes, and in the kinds of social, economic, political, or even aesthetic values that people are likely to develop under altered conditions which we may not be able to foretell.

I am suggesting that, among other things, the factors that mould or change people's attitudes and opinions are sometimes complex and difficult to define; and more importantly, the very factors determining human activities and motivations have a peculiar habit of changing in an unaccountable fashion to frustrate even the most carefully worked out hypotheses. For example, if a sociologist reports that on the basis of his investigation there has been a significant increase in the incidence of suicides among young Singaporeans, and predicts that this trend will rise quite alarmingly over the next twenty years because, among other things, he sees no evidence of lessening tensions or any slowdown in our pace of living; sooner or later some people are going to sit up and do something to improve the unsatisfactory conditions of our rat-race society. You can be sure, too, that those of us who are directly affected by this prediction will not be content to be sitting ducks, waiting helplessly to be overtaken by the "inevitable" hand of fate. Consciously or unconsciously, people are going to do something to reverse the existing trend and, by doing so, falsify the original forecast.

But be that as it may, the scientific prediction of physical phenomena is not the only method open to futurists in their attempt to
understand what the future has in store for us, or how to cope with
various eventualities as and when they arise. They can, and do, resort
to what the Americans call "sketching of scenarios". This simply
means that instead of making a forecast based upon some specific set
of unvarying assumptions and staking one's reputation by it, we attempt instead to figure out what some of the likely consequences
would be if we vary the causal factors involved in the determination of
certain trends or directions in social phenomena. The idea here is to
work out the various possible scenarios, some of which may have no
bearing on reality at all, so that any government or other planning bodies can select the options available to them, especially where the
implementation of certain policies run into difficulties, or where an
unexpected change of the social climate calls for a switch in one's
planning strategies. Thus the advantage of scenario-sketching is that
once we are armed with the relevant data for adopting a range of
different options, we are in a far better position to make the necessary
changes of policy or plan of action should the original idea fail to
produce the kind of results desired.

In the rest of this paper I propose to adopt this principle, where
possible, of sketching out the various possible scenarios affecting Singaporeans as they struggle to adapt to the changing pace of life brought
about by social, economic, technological, and political realities of the
1980s and 1990s.

Let us start off, then, by considering the problem which some in-
fluential people in government have regarded as the serious erosion of
traditional Asian values among the younger generations of Singaporeans. It is noted that as a result of modernization brought about by
industrialization, science, and technology and particularly the influence
of Western lifestyles through the mass media, some of the norms traditionally accepted — such as close family ties, filial piety, love, respect,
and care of one's aged parents, the sanctity of marital ties, thrift, hard
work, and so on — are increasingly being abandoned in favour of a
more self-seeking and materialistic outlook in life, both of which are
the products of modernization and the adoption of Western lifestyles.

Now, as everybody knows, when village crafts and farm work became obsolescent with the advent of industrialization and people began
to move out of the rural areas into the city in search of employment
and greater opportunities in life, the social and emotional ties which
formerly united members of a traditionally extended family became
loosened; and when the mass exodus of young people to the city

took place, the fragmentation of the family into smaller units consisting of husband, wife, and children became a fact of life.

In Singapore, although the development into an industrial economy did not follow exactly the pattern of Western countries, the increasing urbanization brought about by, among other things, a burgeoning population in the aftermath of the Second World War, the rapid expansion of the manufacturing and servicing industries and, particularly, the need to build hundreds of thousands of flatted tenements to maximize the use of scarce land resources, has meant that the preservation of a large extended family had to be abandoned; for large families simply could not be housed in Housing and Development Board flats, while the trend over the years (thanks to the family-planning campaign) has been for smaller families.

As for the younger generations of Singaporeans, it must be remembered that those born after the War have no memories of the privations of hard times; nor can they appreciate the need to uphold the values and traditions of the former generations when times have changed under the impact of economic prosperity and the vogue to adopt the materialistic values and lifestyles of their contemporaries in the West. Unlike the days gone by, the younger generations can nowadays choose to interact exclusively with people of their own age groups; they have their peer groups, their own forms of social entertainment and recreation. The social consequences of these changes in the lifestyles and attitudes of young people have not been entirely desirable, to say the least. On the contrary, modernization has tended to alienate young people from their parents. In particular, they shun their aged parents because the older generations do not speak their language nor share their sentiments for Western fads and fashions.

The widening chasm of non-communication and lack of rapport between the young and the old has meant that, except for those who are still gainfully employed, more and more older people are being relegated to institutional homes for the aged, because their children either do not want them or are simply unable to cope with the expenses of their aged parents. Since it has been projected that by the end of this century there will be something like 10 per cent or about 280,000 people 60 years and above in Singapore, the problem of housing, feeding, and caring for so many economically unproductive people may impose a considerable strain upon our economy.

In recent years, the Government has launched a campaign to persuade young Singaporeans to be more caring towards their aged parents; the Ministry of Finance has granted small income tax reliefs for those who live with their parents; some have resorted to quoting Confucius' teachings in moralizing to the young, while others have condemned

Western values for their corrupting influence. Commendable as these measures are, they will probably not get very far in persuading the majority of young Singaporeans to be more filial and self-sacrificing in their attitude towards their aged parents, because with the high cost of living these days, servants are not only expensive luxuries but difficult to come by. As I see it, the greatly altered conditions of life in Singapore are such that with passing years, the state will somehow have to help out in shouldering the increasing burden of caring for aged Singaporeans.

But of course the situation is not as hopeless as it appears: one can foresee that as the problem of labour shortage in Singapore becomes more acute in the eighties and nineties, both the public and private sectors may find it increasingly necessary to employ the services and expertise of retired Singaporeans. It may, among other things, be necessary to extend the retirement age to 60 and above, so that elderly Singaporeans who are still capable of making useful contributions to the economy would be given the opportunity to provide for themselves. Community centres, schools, vocational institutes, trade union organizations, and commercial companies may find jobs which cater to their needs and as a result of which more older people can be gainfully employed.

Let us pass on to another problem posed by the changing trends in the attitudes of younger generations of Singaporeans to the age-old institution of marriage. It was reported not so long ago that the incidence of divorce has been increasing quite significantly in recent years, and that the highest rate of divorce (something like 40 per cent) occurred among younger married couples between the ages of 19 and 28 or so. The view has been expressed that the higher frequency of divorce among the younger married couples could be attributed to such factors as lack of maturity, hasty decisions, selfishness, and impatience in dealing with the stresses of married life, and so on. If existing trends persist into the eighties and nineties, it is feared that the divorce rates among younger married couples could rise alarmingly, with disastrous consequences to children born of such broken marriages.

While it is true that identifying the causes of a particular phenomenon is essential to the process of solving the problem, I do not feel convinced that we have successfully isolated the crucial factors associated with the rising incidence of divorce among early marriages in Singapore. For one thing, I find it hard to accept that chronological and emotional immaturity are largely responsible for the increasing number of divorces among younger married couples. Most of us know that before the Second World War, marriages in most Asian communities in Singapore were customarily arranged by parents. Boys and girls, when they came of age, were in fact married off earlier than they are today: indeed girls were declared marriageable at 15 or 16 years old, while boys were considered ready to shoulder the responsibilities of husband and fatherhood at around 19 or 20 years of age. As for the problem of lack of emotional maturity, if better education is of any help, young people today ought to be emotionally more mature. Yet the fact remains that most marriages contracted in the days gone by appeared to have been more resistant to frequent breakups. Why is that so?

Several explanations come to mind. To begin with, marriages in the "good" old days were contracted for different reasons, not the least of which was that young couples were not married to each other because they happened to be in love and wanted each other desperately, or that they had known each other for a long period during which friendship had blossomed into affection. Far from it. More often than not the newly-wed couples had never set eyes on each other until the day of the wedding. Marriage was a social and an economic necessity. For those parents who happened to have a large horde of children, the institution of marriage was a convenient method of relieving themselves of the financial burden of having to feed so many mouths, as well as providing some sort of insurance against destitution in old age. For filial piety among children would guarantee that aged parents would always be cared for when they are no longer able to fend for themselves. But apart from the important function of insuring against the infirmities of old age, the institution of marriage, and particularly that of fathering many children in traditional societies, ensured that the family name would be perpetuated, while the provision of adequate manpower in the family helped to increase productivity in the land — in the days when farming was the prevailing way of life.

What about those unavoidable tiffs and frictions which sometimes threaten to break up marriages? One can be sure that married couples in former years had their fair share of family problems, but with this difference: that whenever a marriage appeared to be heading for the rocks, parents as well as relatives would intervene to settle disputes between husband and wife and try to save the marriage in every possible way. The village padre might also be called in to moralize upon the sanctity of marriage; and until the advent of women's liberation movement, wives were usually less assertive and strident about their rights and privileges and more willing to keep a marriage going rather than risk the social stigma of becoming a divorcee.

However, in the vastly changed conditions of life today, all such constraints, which formerly sanctified and sustained even the most unsatisfactory of marriages, have become "old fashioned" and irrelevant. It is no longer necessary for married couples to pledge to remain faithful to each other "for better or for worse, in sickness or in health, until death do part us". So the vacuum created by the disappearance of antiquated values is being filled by what I termed "the philosophy of egoistic hedonism". According to this system of values, my attitude to marriage or any other sort of social relationship with people will always be governed by the question whether such a relationship is conducive to, or enhances, my personal happiness. When it fails to do so, there can be no earthly reason for me to sustain the relationship any longer than it suits me.

If, as I suspect, this is the tacit attitude of most of the younger generation today, the higher rate of divorce among young married couples is not entirely surprising. Indeed it is merely the logical unfolding of the prevailing social norms. Young people are far more fortunate than their counterparts some fifty years ago; they enjoy a greater degree of freedom which comes with better education, better job opportunities, and a higher standard of living. But what of the future?

First a methodological reminder: obviously, the present trend towards a higher divorce rate among young married couples cannot go on increasing exponentially for an indefinite period; otherwise a situation would arise where you have more people getting divorced than there are people getting married. Secondly, people's attitude to the institution of marriage could undergo certain changes with passing time. There is such a thing as changing fashion even in social and moral values, just as fashions in dresses, shoes, handbags, headgear, hairstyles, and furniture change with passing time. For example, during the late fifties and early sixties American youth of that generation decided to repudiate the materialistic value system of the capitalist economy that was America, and all the rat race associated with it. They began to drop out of schools and universities; they gave up lucrative and promising jobs, dispossessed themselves of everything, and went to live in rural communes. Others went to India in search of spiritual enlightenment.

Now I cannot imagine pragmatic and materialistic Singaporeans espousing the kind of values and lifestyles fashionable with American youths of the colourful sixties in either the immediate or foreseeable future; nor, in my opinion, is it desirable in a small and tightly knit society. But I can imagine the sort of scenario in which a later generation of Singaporeans may decide that it would be in their interest as well as that of their society if they revert back to the former system whereby married couples willingly sacrificed their personal interests for the sake of their children and the integrity of the family. This could come about when young people tire of moving from one transitory pairing to another in their endless search for greater personal happiness without necessarily achieving the kind of self-realization they had hoped for. It could also come about through some religious revival (and I hear that this is happening among some groups in Singapore) or simply a nostalgia for some bygone tradition. If and when such a change in social values come about, we can expect that the present high divorce rates among the younger generations will take a downward plunge.

There is one other possible development concerning the change of attitude towards the institution of marriage and the family: should a subsequent generation of young Singaporeans discover that the vogue of moving from one pairing to another in the search for greater personal happiness be illusory, if the costs of bringing up children become prohibitive and involve too much personal sacrifices, they could opt to remain single for as long as it suits them. Indeed some futurists have predicted that the trend in the future is for more people to remain single, because without a family one has fewer responsibilities to bear. Nowadays young people are much more conscious of the need to achieve self-fulfilment or self-realization by pursuing the kind of education they want, the jobs and professions which suit their temperaments, as well as the types of recreations which satisfy their intellectual and emotional needs; and since all the indications are that Singapore's economy will continue to grow with passing years, thus creating more job opportunities, greater social and recreational facilities, it would appear that the attraction of being able to lead a life free from unnecessary social encumbrances (e.g., family responsibilities) would become irresistible for young Singaporeans of the future. Whether this kind of lifestyle, like the trend to experiment with frequent pairings for the purpose of achieving greater personal happiness, will turn out to be a passing fad, only time will tell.

But reference to the materialistic attitude of Singaporeans brings me to another significant aspect of social change which has become increasingly pervasive in recent years. Rapid economic development and rising affluence have encouraged cupidity, as the widespread obsession with money and material gains clearly testifies. The pervasiveness of this preoccupation is, to a large extent, reinforced by the Government's policy of giving priority, if not exclusive emphasis, to the economic aspects of practically all major activities carried out by government departments, statutory bodies, and other organizations run by private enterprise.

Now in the early years of independence when Singapore was fighting for survival, it was necessary for the Government to concentrate its energies almost entirely on developing a viable economy through encouraging trade, promoting industrialization through joint ventures, foreign investment, tourism, and other related activities. Among the urgent problems it had to tackle, serious unemployment caused mainly by the increasing number of school-leavers entering the labour market, population expansion, and threats by underground communist organizations topped the list. Also included among the priorities were the restructuring of the existing system of education, the provision of subsidized apartments for the burgeoning population, the improvement of roads, transport, and other facilities for transforming the Republic into a viable economy.

In the flurry of concerted activities which ensued, the Government naturally gave special attention to those projects which had immediate returns or which directly contributed to economic progress. Similarly, those institutions and persons with the relevant managerial and technical skills who were directly responsible for effecting economic and financial miracles of some sort were all singled out for higher rewards and public recognition. It was not unusual in those days for ministers and other important figures in the Government to make frequent speeches extolling the business acumen, the managerial and administrative ability of successful entrepreneurs and exceptionally gifted civil servants. Even government departments and statutory boards which showed proof of efficiency, profitability, and other evidence of economic growth (e.g., so many miles of road constructed, so many units of flats completed, or so many trees planted) were all given official nods of approval and public recognition.

Naturally under this withering climate of economic brilliance and pervasive money-talk, those institutions, research projects, academic inquiries, or activities of intellectual, artistic, literary, philosophical, and cultural values which, by their very nature, had little or no economic consequences, found it hard to thrive or gain the public attention and support which they badly needed. For while it is relatively easy to specify the criteria of success for a business organization or any other form of economic enterprise in terms of its productivity and profitability, the achievement and status of an artist are not measured by the number of paintings he executes or even sells per year. Nowhere, in my opinion, is the impact of the Government's policy of laying heavy stress on economic development through industrialization and the rapid upgrading of technological skills more apparent than in the manner with which the policies and curricula of our education system have been changed in the last twenty years.

Thus wittingly or unwittingly, the general effect of the Government's policy was to encourage the growth of a materialistic system of values with far-reaching consequences upon the attitudes and lifestyles of most Singaporeans. Here are some of the more obvious ones: the tendency nowadays is to assess the social worth of any person by what is known as his "market value", that is, whether his qualifications or profession enable him to secure a highly paid job complete with every sort of fringe benefits. His social rank is also measured in terms of such status symbols like the kind of home he lives in, the car he drives about, the clubs he joins, and the people he meets and dines with regularly. Ostentation has come to be recognized as the surest means of promoting one's own or one's company image in public, and conspicuous consumption urged on by advertisements, the public media, and the lavish lifestyles of affluent people is the rule rather than the exception. As for the kinds of social activities such as entertainment and recreation in Singapore, since the profit motive is strong, the promotion of the serious cultural, intellectual, literary, and artistic appreciation has been greatly curtailed, simply because cultural activities of the more intellectual sort have rarely been able to obtain large enough audiences to make them financially viable.

It is true that over the years, Singaporeans have become more educated, while tertiary institutions of learning have been producing more graduates. Most of the students pursuing the so-called higher education are of course receiving specialized training to equip them to be engineers, technocrats, business managers, accountants, doctors, computer programmers, and so on. And it is interesting to note that even with respect to the great majority of students admitted to the university faculties which are concerned with what is traditionally known as "liberal education", the prevailing attitude is the strictly pragmatic one of learning simply for the sake of passing examinations and the prospects of obtaining lucrative jobs. So pervasive indeed has the obsession for material gains become, that one cannot help thinking that by and large Singaporeans tend to go through life wearing mental blinkers so that they might concentrate their whole outlook upon the acquisition of material benefits. For this reason, too, most people cannot see, nor perhaps do they care, for the kinds of inquiries which seek, among other things, to enlarge a person's vision and outlook in life, deepen one's understanding of the complexities of human nature, or enhance the scope and intensity of one's aesthetic experience through a better understanding of music, literature, painting, and dancing; because for one thing, there is no money in the cultivation of such intangible human assets, and for another, there is no official campaign to promote gracious living, or grace and charm among a people made dour and tense by the stresses of modernization.

For twenty years at least, the pursuit of a materially better quality of life has been the magnificent obsession of the Government and of most people, so much so that with the exception of important figures in the Government, anyone who has the temerity to advocate a campaign for the nurturing of a more humanistic system of values than the harsh materialism of economic competition that we have been used to, by enriching our mental equipment with some knowledge of literature, drama, poetry, music, or the great philosophical ideas of antiquity, would most certainly be dismissed with arrogant contempt. And the pity about this philistine attitude is that it is born not of a people with a broad and in-depth understanding of the arts, but rather of a rootless, *nouveau riche* people quite ignorant of the art of appreciating things of literary, artistic, musical, and philosophical values. The derisive attitude adopted by some people is simply a rationalization of this ignorance, namely, that what they do not know is perhaps not worth knowing.

But be that as it may, we should not be too eager to criticize Singaporeans for their uncultured attitude, because there has never really been any tradition in our society, from the colonial era up to the present, for the systematic cultivation of artistic, literary, and musical appreciation as a fundamental part of our upbringing or even as a way of life. Our forefathers came here as itinerant immigrants, to make a living, to engage in trade, to get rich if they could, and eventually to return to the land of their ancestors. Like wandering nomads, immigrants who merely "sojourn in the land of strangers" do not readily sprout roots nor, for that matter, develop an indigenous music and literature, both of which are products of settled and leisured people. Since the history of Singapore is relatively short and somewhat turbulent, and the exigency of circumstances has forced us to concentrate our priorities on bread-and-butter matters, we are what we have always been — a nation of traders and shopkeepers. Singapore's history is unlike those of many countries in Europe such as Britain, France, Germany, Italy, Austria, and Russia, where there are well-established institutions such as academies, conservatories, and royal societies for perpetuating interests in the arts and the sciences, where the pursuit of excellence in these endeavours is never despised or disregarded but, on the contrary, continuously patronized and supported by governments, royalty, and the nobility.

According to a recent report in *Time* magazine, the Federal Government of West Germany spends an incredible sum of US$1 billion annually to support some eight hundred museums and art galleries, several hundred theatres, opera houses, orchestras, and other cultural institutions throughout the country. In spite of their formidable economic, scientific, and technological achievements, the Germans are no hard-nosed philistines when it comes to the question of promoting and nurturing things of spiritual and cultural value. In fact, among the older civilizations of Europe and Asia, there has always been a clear recognition that the contributions of artists, poets, musical composers, and even master craftsmen are indispensable cultural assets; and from a historical perspective, it is no exaggeration to say that long after the material wealth and splendour of the civilizations of Nineveh, Mesopotamia, Persia, Greece, and Rome have been forgotten, it is their intellectual, cultural, artistic, and scientific legacies which will be remembered.

I should also mention, in this respect, the example of Japan. In the minds of most people, the Japanese are a nation of united and disciplined people who make it their national policy to pool all their resources together so that they might out-produce the rest of the world in such things as cameras, watches, tape-recorders, transistors, and motor cars — a policy which once provoked the haughty President De Gaulle of France to refer slightingly to the Japanese as "a nation of transistors salesmen". But what many people are probably not aware of is that the Japanese Government zealously protects and preserves its ancient arts, crafts, music, theatres, as well as its literary, philosophical, and religious traditions. In fact they adopt a most unique practice of declaring not only those rare and beautiful artefacts of their heritage as "national treasures" but also living painters, craftsmen, potters, writers, and performing artistes who have made significant contributions in their own fields as "living cultural assets" of Japan. The Japanese take great pains, it is true, to be in the forefront of modern technology, but they are no less enthusiastic about preserving their ancient culture. To mention but one example: the classical *kabuki* drama first performed some time during the fifteenth century is not only alive but thriving and enjoying great popularity with both the young and old in Japan.

By contrast, the classical Chinese operas in Singapore is presently in danger of becoming an extinct art form for lack of public support. In fact the situation has deteriorated to such an extent that those associations which traditionally sponsor street-side *wayangs* on festive days find it necessary to hire some pop bands to punctuate operatic performances with their bizarre singing, much to the amusement of the younger generation and the disgust of older opera fans. What would the consequences be, one wonders, if in an analogous situation the impressario of the New York Metropolitan Opera House had to hire the "Boney M" pop group to sing on the very same night that he is putting up a performance of Wagner's "Tannhauser"?

If Singaporeans have never really enjoyed the benefits of a long tradition in the cultivation of artistic or literary pursuits and the appreciation of such things in the past, we may have expected that the contemporary scene would at least offer some encouragement in these directions. Unfortunately this is not so, for as we have alluded to earlier on, the deep and pervasive preoccupation with material gains makes it difficult to rally sufficient public support and recognition of the value of cultural pursuits.

Our education system is not of much help either, since over the last two decades or so, the policy has been to load the curriculum heavily in favour of the training of skills related to economic development through industrialization. To make the matter more discouraging, it is a fact that the nurturing of mature knowledge and skills pertaining to fine arts, literature, and music takes a very long time (measured in decades), with the further proviso that no quick or tangible returns can be expected either in the form of a cultural renaissance or bountiful financial gains of any sort. Hence, if one is thinking of fast returns in the form of dollars and cents or other material equivalents, one would do better by investing one's financial resources in the training of those types of skills and expertise which have immediate market value. And that, in my opinion, has been the policy of the Government and of most people in Singapore.

It would appear, then, that the prospects facing those concerned with the pursuit of non-material and non-economic values are bleak — that is, if we assume that the prevailing trend of crass materialism and philistinism is likely to remain a permanent feature of our society. But this need not necessarily be so; for if one should draw a lesson from the history of past civilizations, one will find that some of the greatest achievements in art, literature, music, philosophy, and even architecture coincided with eras of political greatness and economic prosperity. For example, during the T'ang Dynasty (A.D. 618—908) in China a succession of emperors with strong personalities and aggressive ambitions led to the expansion of the Chinese Empire until about A.D. 642 during the reign of Tai-tsung; it stretched from the Yellow Sea in the east to Lake Aral in the far west of Central Asia. This was also the era of great prosperity and intense literary activities culminating in the rise of such poets as Wang Wei, Li Po, Tu Fu, and Po-Chu-i. It also saw the development of the Buddhist religion and the blossoming of Buddhist art such as China had never seen before or after.

In the same way, if one examines the history of the Roman Empire, it will soon be obvious that when Augustus ascended the throne in Rome at about the beginning of the Christian Era, the Empire had reached the zenith of political power, territorial extent, and economic strength. It also happened, whether by accident or by design, that this was the era of great Roman jurists and philosophers such as Cicero and Seneca. It encouraged the revival of interest in Greek drama, literature, philosophy, architecture, and sculpture, and some of the finest of Roman art is attributed to this period.

As for Italy of the fifteenth and sixteenth centuries, the rise of the rich and powerful Medici family in Florence and the advent of warrior-popes imbued with political and temporal ambitions provided the country with a succession of great art patrons and the development of rival schools of excellent painters, sculptors, craftsmen, architects, and particularly that unique species of "renaissance scholars" noted for their originality of thinking and the sweep of their intellect. Few people today remember, or even care to remember, the names of the various popes and noble families who sponsored the growth of art in Rome and Florence. But the names of Leonardo da Vinci, Michelangelo, Raphael, and Bellini are well remembered.

If the lesson of past history is any guide to the future, we ought not to decry the crass materialism of Singaporeans; for we can expect that if the future continues to bode well for us, we will by then have attained a standard of material comfort and the luxury of greater leisure which make more people more willing to cultivate a greater awareness for things of cultural and spiritual values. If and when that day comes about, and literary and artistic endeavours no longer need to go abegging for want of an audience, then those of us who have had to struggle so fruitlessly to make a living in the name of art, culture, or self-realization would have cause to be satisfied that we kept the beacon of hope alive through an era when everything had seemed so dark and so hopelessly discouraging.

# 12

## Towards a Creative Society

### William S.W. Lim

The year 2000 is not so far away. Many of us here are likely to be still alive, unless the world is destroyed by a nuclear holocaust. Owing to scarcity of land and the structure of the economy, the well-being of Singapore is closely interlinked with and affected by major developments in the international economy. Each or a combination of the following three major events can have serious effects on and near-disastrous consequences for Singapore: (1) global shortage of food grain due to population explosion in Third World countries and mismanagement of agricultural production, (2) acute shortage of essential mineral resources mainly because of unregulated and escalating consumption by the economically advanced countries, and (3) economic chaos arising from continuous inflation, high rate of unemployment, and economic stagnation in the Western countries and Japan due to the inability of these countries to restructure their priorities to meet changing conditions. Unfortunately, it is outside the capacity of Singapore to control or effectively influence the direction of these global developments. We can only hope that the survival instinct of the respective governments and their people will collectively ensure that these problems will not be permitted to escalate to drastic global dimensions.

There are too many variables and uncertainties in trying to project Singapore towards the year 2000. The projection can at best only be based on probabilities. Furthermore, such attempts are always subjective, and therefore ideologically biased and value-loaded. In this paper, I shall briefly identify the important changing global scenario and then present my argument why it is desirable for Singapore to prepare the groundwork towards a creative society now in order that we can move towards the twenty-first century with confidence. I do not doubt that there are other options available. The critical issue we must ask ourselves is — Will the younger generation today be satisfied with the kind of future we are attempting to build for them? If they are not, they will reject the option chosen. This process of rejection will most certainly be a very painful one.

*Changing Global Scenario*

As we move towards the year 2000, a changing power balance will most likely take place. The most drastic development will be the emergence of China as a major industrial power. This is assuming that the target of the Four Modernizations can be partially achieved. At the same time, there will be a relative decline in the present economically advanced countries, particularly Western Europe and Japan. In the time span of twenty years, there will certainly be many changes and developments in each country. However, the collective impact of the smaller countries in the Asian region will be relatively small compared to the changes likely to take place in China and Japan.

Though the rate of global population increase is slowing down, the population explosion will cause a greater increase in the cost of food in relation to that of industrial products. Notwithstanding higher productivity in agriculture, food production will be substantially limited by the availability of agricultural land. The members of the Organization of Petroleum Exporting Countries (OPEC) have already shown how to ensure that oil prices can increase faster than imported industrial products. It is very conceivable the same will apply to food prices. It is hoped that Third World countries will give top priority to the agricultural sector and offer the millions of peasants a better deal. The present granaries in the United States, Canada, and Australia cannot continue to meet the food deficiency of other countries.

If a serious shortage of basic non-renewable resources is to be avoided, the economically advanced countries must learn to minimize wasteful consumption. There will be a greater demand for these resources, owing to the population increase, industrialization, and higher standards of living in Third World countries. The escalating cost of energy is particularly serious. The use of solar, water, and wind energy as well as bio-gas, etc., will soon be commercially competitive and can provide a considerable amount of energy. It is likely that there will still be many unresolved technical problems related to the large-scale use of coal as well as nuclear energy. In the year 2000, the world will still depend heavily on oil as a major energy source.

Industrial and technological development will occur in most Third World countries. Exports of technologically-oriented industrial products are likely to be increasingly competitive. As technology becomes universally available, most countries can establish industries to satisfy their own basic needs, irrespective whether these countries have achieved a high level of economic development, a high per capita income, and more equitable income distribution. Sophisticated technology is expensive and generally needs large capital input and highly skilled and trained manpower. The demand for these products will increase. However, they are unlikely to achieve the same importance in international trade as that of industrial products from the economically advanced countries.

During the next two decades, the economically advanced countries will have completed the painful process of restructuring their societies. The obsession for economic growth will have diminished. Attention will be concentrated on providing the social and cultural environment for personal fulfilment and improving the quality of life for all citizens. In the process, tourism will continue to increase, though the expectation of tourists will be very different. The experience of a different cultural environment and meaningful contact with local people will become increasingly important. Academic achievement, professional skills, and creative ability will be in great demand. Objects of daily use, such as clothes, furniture, toys, etc., which are well designed will become important export items. There will also be a greater demand for good books, paintings, music, and films.

### Towards a Creative Environment

With a dedicated and intelligent political leadership, an efficient and honest bureaucracy, and a hardworking and responsive population, Singapore has achieved much during the 1960s and 1970s. To meet the challenges of the eighties, the Government has initiated many forward-planning actions. The most important policy changes which have been initiated today are to upgrade the skills of workers, to attract labour-intensive high-technology industries, and to increase the living standard of the working class. At the same time, the need to maintain the work ethics is strongly emphasized.

By the year 2000, it is most likely that Singapore will have achieved its objective of establishing itself as an important centre for labour-intensive high-technology industries. Singapore will also have enhanced its present position as a regional centre for tourism, trade, banking, and transportation. It can be envisaged that the steady growth of its economy will raise the per capita income and living standard very appreciably.

A free-enterprise economy, which depends on technology, trade, and commerce, must inevitably orientate itself towards the accumulation of wealth. In such a system, the success of an individual is measured by his ability to make money. The work ethics is maintained only because of the need to make sufficient money in order to obtain the various forms of enjoyment which money can buy. Consumerism is the basic ingredient of his lifestyle. Education is just a convenient passport to a well-paid job, and work is often an uneventful experience to be tolerated.

When the basic material needs are satisfied, people will demand more leisure, more recreation, and most of all the chance to live a satisfying, enjoyable, and happy life. Material wealth can provide more leisure and recreation. But happiness cannot be achieved through consumerism. The human spirit cannot be totally satisfied with material opulence. The quality of life can be enhanced when work is enjoyable and not a chore, when work is the deliberate choice through which one achieves fuller life-experience, and when work is apportioned with responsibility and is performed with pride.

## Creative Arts

In a creative society, a great variety of job options are available, particularly for those who are capable of and are interested in being artistically creative and "doing their own thing". Many will attempt to become artists, writers, musicians, film makers, entertainers, etc. Initially, they must all be encouraged in order to discover the talented few. In this talent scouting, it must be remembered that creative talent cannot be measured by IQ tests or academic qualifications. If creativity is to develop, the creators must have the means to meet their basic material needs. Only a minority will succeed and they may take a long time to gain recognition. Some will go on trying, while others will give up after repeated failures. Fortunately, the small successful minority can effectively enrich the cultural life of the society.

This analysis will also apply to other artistically-related creative occupations, such as architecture, interior design, industrial and graphic design, and others. If the design standards of these occupations are to be raised, it is essential that the potentially talented practitioners must be prepared to offer their best in order to discover and develop their own potential talent. The temptation to turn commercial and become financially successful is always there, but must certainly be discouraged.

Creativity is not a monopoly based on social class, occupation, wealth, or formal education. A creative person is a liberated individual. To innovate and create something new and different, he can respond to and communicate with other creative individuals, even if they belong to different fields of activity. His creative ideas may be recognized by his peers and colleagues outside his own country. But his work may not be accepted by his contemporaries or the establishment. For a creative environment to exist, there must be a high degree of tolerance and acceptance of controversy and criticism.

## Physical Environment

A creative physical environment must relate to people. The international style of modern architecture is dehumanizing and must be discarded or at least substantially modified. We must produce buildings which can be understood by and related to people. Architecture must be humanized. There must be bright colours, exciting forms, and definable spaces as well as culturally-related symbols, especially in public and religious buildings. Much of our physical environment must be preserved and rehabilitated in order to provide a visual expression of our historical and cultural heritage. Preservation should include not only individual buildings of architectural and historical significance but also our vernacular architecture, such as the numerous rows of terrace houses, the magnificent old bungalows, the riverside godowns, and places of social, cultural, and historical association, as well as whole areas in the older parts of what has escaped decades of indiscriminate destruction.

## Educational Policy

Educational policy must be flexible enough to provide options for students to develop to their full potential. Late developers should be given the opportunity to fulfil their ambition at their own pace. In the school curriculum, literature and the visual arts must be given the importance they deserve. If our students are not trained to produce or at least appreciate good literature and the visual arts, it will not be possible for a creative cultural environment to be developed. Institutions of higher learning must provide the necessary facilities for courses in music, fine arts, interior design, graphic arts, etc. We need to broaden the opportunities of admission to higher education for those who want to continue studying, as well as to provide opportunities for those who are already working. Part-time courses, open university facilities, and other educational arrangements should be made available.

## Participation

School children and the younger generation must be encouraged to actively participate in decision-making. Their suggestions and criticism must be tolerated and considered seriously. It is realized that for a society to function, certain values and a code of conduct need to be inculcated and even enforced. However, they must be exercised with extreme caution and constraint. Active participation at all levels must be encouraged and introduced. It should become an integral part of our cultural values and way of life.

Participation may take different forms in educational institutions, in industries, in the service sector, and in the different levels of government policy implementation. The scope of participation is very broad, and should only be limited when its action adversely affects the well-being of others. Every child can be encouraged to be an active participant in the family. Students should actively participate in the educational process and workers in the work process. With participation, people are more involved and committed to what they are doing. It may not lead to better efficiency, and it may even be temporarily counter-productive and disruptive. However, the benefits of the experience to the participants are immeasurable. In the long run, participation gives satisfaction, develops responsibility, confidence, and pride.

## Work Ethics

In the year 2000, will Singapore become a country of labour opt-outs or work-a-holics? From the experience of the economically advanced countries, there is an unavoidable erosion of the work ethics when the living standard is improved beyond a certain level. Some may ask what is going to happen to the work ethics in a participatory and creative society. I submit that the work ethics is likely to remain, but will take different forms. The perception of and attitudes towards work will be different. Participation heightens the sense of involvement and collective responsibility. People will work hard, not because they are ordered to do so or even just for the money. At its best, work like leisure becomes enjoyable and contributes to the life-experiences of the individuals.

## Cultural Values

Being a global city, Singapore is continually subjected to external influences from all directions. At present, we are still consciously trying to establish our roots in the cultural past of our ancestors. Subconsciously, there is also an attempt to identify with the cultural values of colonial Britain. It may be necessary that we must learn from history, but it is a sterile exercise to attempt to codify our value system from our past. We must not create a "plastic culture", that is, a culture with respectable appearances but incapable of evolution. In my view, Singapore's culture is alive and dynamic. It is rapidly changing. It is expressed in many ways, including the way we dress, speak, and behave and the variety of food we eat as well as our values and lifestyles. If we lack an exciting cultural environment today, it is because society is obsessed with technology, economic development, and consumerism. Singapore has given very little attention or encouragement to the creative arts. We need to have continuous creative inputs to express the mood, the feeling, the changing values, and perception of our people.

## Conclusion

Finally, I wish to state that I do not believe in the long-term viability of a highly competitive consumer-orientated society. When the basic material needs are generally satisfied, there will be an increasing demand for a better quality of life, for more job options, for more active participation, and for opportunities to enjoy and be involved in creative occupation. Society is in continuous evolution. Each generation will set and define its goals. Man can never be satisfied with just materialism and only what money can buy. He will continue to seek personal fulfilment and happiness through a wide range of spiritual and creative experience.

The creative society is also a humane society, where income distribution is more equitable, and where the citizens are more honest, caring, and friendly. Such a society will not accept a high degree of social discipline and may not be the most economically productive. The idea of a creative society may appear idealistic to some and disturbing to others. The younger generation is likely to consider it the most desirable option. Let us be tolerant and allow others their dreams.

# Notes on Contributors

*R. S. Bhathal* is Director of the Singapore Science Centre.

*Chan Heng Chee* is Associate Professor in the Department of Political Science, National University of Singapore.

*Chia Wai Hon* is a Lecturer in the Department of Art Education, Institute of Education.

*Ho Wing Meng* is Associate Professor in the Department of Philosophy, National University of Singapore.

*Lim Chee Onn* is Minister without Portfolio and Secretary-General of the Singapore National Trades Union Congress.

*William S. W. Lim* is a partner of DP Architects Pte. Ltd.

*Liu Thai-Ker* is Chief Executive Officer of the Housing and Development Board.

*Pang Eng Fong* is Director of the Economic Research Centre, National University of Singapore.

*S. Rajaratnam* is Second Deputy Prime Minister (Foreign Affairs).

*Saw Swee-Hock* is Professor of Statistics in the Department of Economics and Statistics, National University of Singapore.

*Tay Sin-Yan* is a Consultant in the Asian Development Bank.

*Wong Hock Boon* is Senior Professor of Medicine and Director of the School of Post-Graduate Medical Studies.